VB.NET CODE WARRIOR

Working with DAO

By Richard Thomas Edwards

CONTENTS

WELCOME TO DAO

The Godfather of Data Access

I CONSIDER DAO – which means Data Access Objects -TO BE THE GODFATHER OF DATA ACCESS BECAUSE IT HAS BEEN THE WAY TO CONNECT TO AND CREATE DATABASES, TABLES AND STORED PROCEEDURES YEARS BEFORE I WENT TO WORK FOR MICROSOFT.

In fact, knowing it helped me to land my first job at Microsoft.

But there was something coming through the development pipeline that made every attempt of dethroning it: Active X Data Objects.

Their reasoning was quite simple, Do the same thing in memory and it will be much faster.

Well, that worked until hard drives – SSDs and the newest kid on the block, USB SSDs – no longer made the speed distinction a factor and, once again, DAO is back in the spotlight.

LET'S VENTURE BACKWARDS IN TIME FOR JUST A MOMENT

Anyone who remembers the wild, wild Microsoft days knows what the worlds DLL HELL meant. Those were the good old days, right?

R.I.P to them!

Anyway, back then we had things like DAO.DBEngine.25–AKA the thunker – which served to support the notion that 16-bit and 32-bit versions of data access. It was Microsoft's way of appeasing the gods. And, of course that was short lived when

Microsoft grew up fast and started compromising quality support for higher profit margins.

So, by 1998, DAO.DBEngine.35, a 32-bit only Database Engine had been created and most us working in Technical Support were pretty sure ADO was going to replace it.

It didn't. In fact, when VB.NET came out with DAO.DBEngine.36, we very quickly learned why.

In fact, I wrote two KB Articles on the issue. Then installation and the remove of Access 97 removed the key in the registry that made the VB.NET development environment effectively useless with respect to DAO.

So, after that fiasco, most of us were pretty sure DAO was on the way out.

We were, once again, wrong.

Office 2007 shipped with DAO.DBEngine.120.

BACK TO THE FUTURE

Today, after installing Office 365, I find no changes in the COM version of DAO. The COM version supports dbVersion120. However, the .Net version of COM supports up to dbVersion150 according to the Object Browser. I'm not even sure that is possible considering the same functionality found in the .Net COM version should be the same.

For right now, none of this really matters as we need to focus on connecting to DAO and what you can do with what you have installed.

WHAT DAO CAN DO FOR YOU

First, DAO supports local as well as remote connections.

Second, you can connect to a database using:

There are ISAMS -- Indexed Sequential Access Method – well as all the ODBC – Open Database Connectivity – drivers including SQL Server that can be used along with the standard connectivity using database naming. Below are some examples of what is meant:

STANDARD DATABASE CONNECTION

Please keep in mind that you could use DAO.DBEngine.35, DAO.DBEngine.36 or DAO.DBEngine.120 with all the below examples.

```
Dim Filename As String
Filename = "C:\Program Files (x86)\Microsoft Visual Studio\VB98\Nwind.mdb"
Dim DBEngine As Object = CreateObject("DAO.DBEngine.36")
Dim db As Object = DBEngine.OpenDatabase(filename)
```

A ISAM CONNECTION USING DAO

It works like this:

```
Filename = "C:\ISAMS\Text"
Dim DBEngine As Object = CreateObject("DAO.DBEngine.36")
Dim db As Object = DBEngine.OpenDatabase(filename, , , "Text; hdr=yes;")
```

And the Query:

```
Dim rs As Object = db.OpenRecordset("Select * from (Myfile.csv)")
```

TO CREATE A DAO DATABASE

```
dbLangGeneral = ";LANGID=0x0409;CP=1252;COUNTRY=0"

dbVersion30 = 32
dbVersion40 = 64
dbVersion120 = 128

Dim DBEngine As Object = CreateObject("DAO.DBEngine.120")
Dim db As Object = dbEngine.CreateDatabase("C:\MyFirst.accdb", dbLangGeneral, dbVersion120)

Dim DBEngine As Object = CreateObject("DAO.DBEngine.36")
```

```
Dim db As Object = dbEngine.CreateDatabase("C:\MyFirst.mdb", dbLangGeneral, dbVersion40)

Dim DBEngine As Object = CreateObject("DAO.DBEngine.35")
Dim db As Object = dbEngine.CreateDatabase("C:\MyFirst.mdb", dbLangGeneral, dbVersion30)
```

TO OPEN THE DATABASE

```
Dim DBEngine As Object = CreateObject("DAO.DBEngine.120")
Dim db As Object = dbEngine.OpenDatabase("C:\MyFirst.accdb")

Dim DBEngine As Object = CreateObject("DAO.DBEngine.36")
Dim db As Object = dbEngine.OpenDatabase("C:\MyFirst.mdb")

Dim DBEngine As Object = CreateObject("DAO.DBEngine.35")
Dim db As Object = dbEngine.OpenDatabase("C:\MyFirst.mdb")
```

CREATE AND POPULATE TABLE

```
Dim tbldef as Object = db.CreateTableDef("Process_Properties")
For x = 0 To rs1. Fields.Count-1
  Dim fld as Object = tbldef .CreateField(Prop.Name, 12)
  fld.AllowZeroLength = true
  tbldef.Fields.Append(fld)
Next
db.TableDefs.Append(tbldef)
```

I use 12 or a memo field because I don't want to have to worry about the data type or the size of the information I'm passing in. This could become problematic if I didn't.

```
Dim rs As Object = db.OpenRecordset("Processes_Properties")
Do While rs1.EOF = false
  rs.AddNew()
  for x = 0 to rs1.Fields.Count-1
    rs.Fields(x).Value = rs1.Fields(x).Value
  Next
  rs.Update()
  rs1.MoveFirst()
Loop
```

OPEN RECORDSET

Dim rs As Object = db.OpenRecordset("Select * From Processes_Properties", Exclusive:=False)

Or:

Dim rs As Object = db.OpenRecordset("Processes_Properties")

TABLES AND VIEWS

At this point you're probably scratching your head trying to figure out how I went from creating a query against a known table. Well, in DAO, it can't get much easier than this:

```
Dim DBEngine As Object = CreateObject("DAO.DBEngine.36")
Dim db As Object =  DBEngine.OpenDatabase("D:\NWind.mdb")

For each tbldef in db.TableDefs
  If mid(tbldef.Name, 1, 4) <> "MSys" then
    WScript.Echo(tbldef.Name)
  End If
Next
```

The Results:

Categories
Customers
Employees
Order Details
Orders
Products
Shippers
Suppliers

As for Views:

```
Dim DBEngine As Object = CreateObject("DAO.DBEngine.36")
Dim db As Object =  DBEngine.OpenDatabase("D:\NWind.mdb")

For each QDef in db.QueryDefs
  WScript.Echo(tbldef.Name)
Next
```

The Results:

Category Sales for 1995
Current Product List
Invoices
Order Details Extended
Order Subtotals
Product Sales for 1995
Products Above Average Price
Quarterly Orders
Sales by Category
Ten Most Expensive Products

Okay, so now you know something about connection strings and how to get table and view information, it is time to start using that information to create an assortment of user outputs which just might make you and your boss get some warm and fuzzy feelings.

ASP CODE

THERE IS NOTING FANTASIC ABOUT CREATING ASP OR ASPX WEB PAGES. In fact, additional hoops must be jumped - web site where you can cut and paste what you just created from here is one of them. So, with that said, I've added enough bells and whistles into the code structure to make it worth your while. Here's what is in store for you:

- Report View
  - Horizontal
    - None
    - Button
    - Combobox
    - Div
    - Link
    - Listbox
    - Span
    - Textarea
    - Textbox
  - Vertical
    - None
    - Button
    - Combobox
    - Div
    - Link

        - Listbox
        - Span
        - Textarea
        - Textbox

- Table View
    - Horizontal
        - None
        - Button
        - Combobox
        - Div
        - Link
        - Listbox
        - Span
        - Textarea
        - Textbox
    - Vertical
        - None
        - Button
        - Combobox
        - Div
        - Link
        - Listbox
        - Span
        - Textarea
        - Textbox

```
Dim ws As Object = CreateObject("WScript.Shell")
Dim fso As Object = CreateObject("Scripting.FileSystemObject")
Dim txtstream As Object =fso.OpenTextFile(ws.CurrentDirectory + "\Products.asp", 2, true, -2)
txtstream.WriteLine("<html>")
txtstream.WriteLine("<head>")
txtstream.WriteLine("<title>" + Tablename + "</title>")
#Add Stylesheet here
txtstream.WriteLine("<body>")
txtstream.WriteLine("</br>")
```

Horizontal Reports

```
txtstream.WriteLine("<table border=0 cellspacing=3 cellpadding=3>")
txtstream.WriteLine("<%")
txtstream.WriteLine("Response.Write(""<tr>"" + vbcrlf)")
For x = 0 to rs.Fields.Count-1
   txtstream.WriteLine("Response.Write(""<th style="" font-family:Calibri, Sans-Serif;font-size: 12px;color:darkred;"" align='left' nowrap='nowrap'>" + rs.Fields(x).Name + "</th>"" + vbcrlf)")
Next
txtstream.WriteLine("Response.Write(""</tr>"" + vbcrlf)")
Do While(rs.EOF = false)
   txtstream.WriteLine("Response.Write(""<tr>"" + vbcrlf)")
   For x = 0 to rs.Fields.Count-1
```

NONE

```
         txtstream.WriteLine("Response.Write(""<td style=""font-family:Calibri, Sans-Serif;font-size: 12px;color:navy;"" align='left' nowrap='nowrap'>" + rs.Fields(x).Value + "</td>"" + vbcrlf)")
```

Button

```
txtstream.WriteLine("Response.Write(""<td style=""font-family:Calibri, Sans-Serif;font-size: 12px;color:navy;"" align='left' nowrap='true'><button style='width:100%;' value ='" + rs.Fields(x).Value + "'>" + rs.Fields(x).Value + "</button></td>"" + vbcrlf)")
```

COMBOBOX

```
txtstream.WriteLine("Response.Write(""<td style=""font-family:Calibri, Sans-Serif;font-size: 12px;color:navy;"" align='left' nowrap='true'><select><option value = """" + rs.Fields(x).Value + """">" + rs.Fields(x).Value + "</option></select></td>"" + vbcrlf)")
```

DIV

```
txtstream.WriteLine("Response.Write(""<td style=""font-family:Calibri, Sans-Serif;font-size: 12px;color:navy;"" align='left' nowrap='true'><div>" + rs.Fields(x).Value + "</div></td>"" + vbcrlf)")
```

LINK

```
txtstream.WriteLine("Response.Write(""<td style=""font-family:Calibri, Sans-Serif;font-size: 12px;color:navy;"" align='left' nowrap='true'><a href='" + rs.Fields(x).Value + "'>" + rs.Fields(x).Value + "</a></td>"" + vbcrlf)")
```

LISTBOX

```
txtstream.WriteLine("Response.Write(""<td style=""font-family:Calibri, Sans-Serif;font-size: 12px;color:navy;"" align='left' nowrap='true'><select multiple><option value = """" + rs.Fields(x).Value + """">" + rs.Fields(x).Value + "</option></select></td>"" + vbcrlf)")
```

SPAN

```
txtstream.WriteLine("Response.Write(""<td style=""font-family:Calibri, Sans-Serif;font-size: 12px;color:navy;"" align='left' nowrap='true'><span>" + rs.Fields(x).Value + "</span></td>"" + vbcrlf)")
```

TEXTAREA

```
        txtstream.WriteLine("Response.Write(""<td style=""font-family:Calibri, Sans-Serif;font-size: 12px;color:navy;"" align='left' nowrap='true'><textarea>" + rs.Fields(x).Value + "</textarea></td>"" + vbcrlf)")
```

TEXTBOX

```
        txtstream.WriteLine("Response.Write(""<td style=""font-family:Calibri, Sans-Serif;font-size: 12px;color:navy;"" align='left' nowrap='true'><input type=text value=""" + rs.Fields(x).Value + """></input></td>"" + vbcrlf)")
      Next
      txtstream.WriteLine("Response.Write(""</tr>"" + vbcrlf)")
      rs.MoveNext
  Loop
  txtstream.WriteLine("%>")
  txtstream.WriteLine("</table>")
  txtstream.WriteLine("</body>")
  txtstream.WriteLine("</html>")
  txtstream.Close()
```

Vertical Reports

```
  txtstream.WriteLine("<table border=0 cellspacing=3 cellpadding=3>")
  txtstream.WriteLine("<%")
  For x = 0 to rs.Fields.Count-1
      txtstream.WriteLine("Response.Write(""<tr><th style="" font-family:Calibri, Sans-Serif;font-size: 12px;color:darkred;"" align='left' nowrap='nowrap'>" + rs.Fields(x).Name + "</th>"" + vbcrlf)")
      rs.MoveFirst()
      Do While(rs.EOF = false)
       txtstream.WriteLine("Response.Write(""<td style=""font-family:Calibri, Sans-Serif;font-size: 12px;color:navy;"">" + rs.Fields(x).Value + "</td>"" + vbcrlf)")
```

NONE

```
        txtstream.WriteLine("Response.Write(""<td style=""font-family:Calibri, Sans-Serif;font-size: 12px;color:navy;"" align='left' nowrap='nowrap'>" + rs.Fields(x).Value + "</td>"" + vbcrlf)")
```

Button

```
txtstream.WriteLine("Response.Write(""<td style=""font-family:Calibri, Sans-Serif;font-size: 12px;color:navy;"" align='left' nowrap='true'><button style='width:100%;' value ='" + rs.Fields(x).Value + "'>" + rs.Fields(x).Value + "</button></td>"" + vbcrlf)")
```

Combobox

```
txtstream.WriteLine("Response.Write(""<td style=""font-family:Calibri, Sans-Serif;font-size: 12px;color:navy;"" align='left' nowrap='true'><select><option value = """" + rs.Fields(x).Value + """">" + rs.Fields(x).Value + "</option></select></td>"" + vbcrlf)")
```

Div

```
txtstream.WriteLine("Response.Write(""<td style=""font-family:Calibri, Sans-Serif;font-size: 12px;color:navy;"" align='left' nowrap='true'><div>" + rs.Fields(x).Value + "</div></td>"" + vbcrlf)")
```

Link

```
txtstream.WriteLine("Response.Write(""<td style=""font-family:Calibri, Sans-Serif;font-size: 12px;color:navy;"" align='left' nowrap='true'><a href='" + rs.Fields(x).Value + "'>" + rs.Fields(x).Value + "</a></td>"" + vbcrlf)")
```

Listbox

```
txtstream.WriteLine("Response.Write(""<td style=""font-family:Calibri, Sans-Serif;font-size: 12px;color:navy;"" align='left' nowrap='true'><select multiple><option value = """" + rs.Fields(x).Value + """">" + rs.Fields(x).Value + "</option></select></td>"" + vbcrlf)")
```

Span

```
txtstream.WriteLine("Response.Write(""<td style=""font-family:Calibri, Sans-Serif;font-size: 12px;color:navy;"" align='left' nowrap='true'><span>" + rs.Fields(x).Value + "</span></td>"" + vbcrlf)")
```

Textarea

```
txtstream.WriteLine("Response.Write(""<td style=""font-family:Calibri, Sans-Serif;font-size: 12px;color:navy;"" align='left' nowrap='true'><textarea>" + rs.Fields(x).Value + "</textarea></td>"" + vbcrlf)")
```

Textbox

```
        txtstream.WriteLine("Response.Write(""<td style=""font-family:Calibri, Sans-Serif;font-size: 12px;color:navy;"" align='left' nowrap='true'><input type=text value=""" + rs.Fields(x).Value + """></input></td>"" + vbcrlf)")
        rs.MoveNext
       loop
     txtstream.WriteLine("Response.Write(""</tr>"" + vbcrlf)")
Next
txtstream.WriteLine("%>")
txtstream.WriteLine("</table>")
txtstream.WriteLine("</body>")
txtstream.WriteLine("</html>")
txtstream.Close()
```

Horizontal Tables

```
txtstream.WriteLine("<table style='border:Double;border-width:1px;border-color:navy;' rules=all frames=both cellpadding=2 cellspacing=2 Width=0>")
txtstream.WriteLine("<%")
txtstream.WriteLine("Response.Write(""<tr>"" + vbcrlf)")
For x = 0 to rs.Fields.Count-1
   txtstream.WriteLine("Response.Write(""<th style="" font-family:Calibri, Sans-Serif;font-size: 12px;color:darkred;"" align='left' nowrap='nowrap'>" + rs.Fields(x).Name + "</th>"" + vbcrlf)")

Next
```

```
txtstream.WriteLine("Response.Write(""</tr>"" + vbcrlf)")
Do While(rs.EOF = false)
  txtstream.WriteLine("Response.Write(""<tr>"" + vbcrlf)")
    For x = 0 to rs.Fields.Count-1
```

NONE

```
txtstream.WriteLine("Response.Write(""<td style=""font-family:Calibri, Sans-Serif;font-size: 12px;color:navy;"" align='left' nowrap='nowrap'>" + rs.Fields(x).Value + "</td>"" + vbcrlf)")
```

Button

```
txtstream.WriteLine("Response.Write(""<td style=""font-family:Calibri, Sans-Serif;font-size: 12px;color:navy;"" align='left' nowrap='true'><button style='width:100%;' value ='" + rs.Fields(x).Value + "'>" + rs.Fields(x).Value + "</button></td>"" + vbcrlf)")
```

COMBOBOX

```
txtstream.WriteLine("Response.Write(""<td style=""font-family:Calibri, Sans-Serif;font-size: 12px;color:navy;"" align='left' nowrap='true'><select><option value = """" + rs.Fields(x).Value + """">" + rs.Fields(x).Value + "</option></select></td>"" + vbcrlf)")
```

DIV

```
txtstream.WriteLine("Response.Write(""<td style=""font-family:Calibri, Sans-Serif;font-size: 12px;color:navy;"" align='left' nowrap='true'><div>" + rs.Fields(x).Value + "</div></td>"" + vbcrlf)")
```

LINK

```
txtstream.WriteLine("Response.Write(""<td style=""font-family:Calibri, Sans-Serif;font-size: 12px;color:navy;"" align='left' nowrap='true'><a href='" + rs.Fields(x).Value + "'>" + rs.Fields(x).Value + "</a></td>"" + vbcrlf)")
```

LISTBOX

```
txtstream.WriteLine("Response.Write(""<td style=""font-family:Calibri, Sans-Serif;font-size: 12px;color:navy;"" align='left' nowrap='true'><select multiple><option value = """" + rs.Fields(x).Value + """">" + rs.Fields(x).Value + "</option></select></td>"" + vbcrlf)")
```

SPAN

```
txtstream.WriteLine("Response.Write(""<td style=""font-family:Calibri, Sans-Serif;font-size: 12px;color:navy;"" align='left' nowrap='true'><span>" + rs.Fields(x).Value + "</span></td>"" + vbcrlf)")
```

TEXTAREA

```
txtstream.WriteLine("Response.Write(""<td style=""font-family:Calibri, Sans-Serif;font-size: 12px;color:navy;"" align='left' nowrap='true'><textarea>" + rs.Fields(x).Value + "</textarea></td>"" + vbcrlf)")
```

TEXTBOX

```
txtstream.WriteLine("Response.Write(""<td style=""font-family:Calibri, Sans-Serif;font-size: 12px;color:navy;"" align='left' nowrap='true'><input type=text value="""" + rs.Fields(x).Value + """"></input></td>"" + vbcrlf)")

        txtstream.WriteLine("Response.Write(""</tr>"" + vbcrlf)")
        rs.MoveNext

    txtstream.WriteLine("%>")
    txtstream.WriteLine("</table>")
    txtstream.WriteLine("</body>")
    txtstream.WriteLine("</html>")
    txtstream.Close()
```

Vertical Tables

```
txtstream.WriteLine("<table style='border:Double;border-width:1px;border-color:navy;' rules=all frames=both cellpadding=2 cellspacing=2 Width=0>")
```

```
txtstream.WriteLine("<%")

For x = 0 to rs.Fields.Count-1
    txtstream.WriteLine("Response.Write(""<tr><th style="" font-family:Calibri, Sans-Serif;font-size: 12px;color:darkred;"" align='left' nowrap='nowrap'>" + rs.Fields(x).Name + "</th>"" + vbcrlf)")
    rs.MoveFirst()
    Do While(rs.EOF = false)
     txtstream.WriteLine("Response.Write(""<td style=""font-family:Calibri, Sans-Serif;font-size: 12px;color:navy;"">" + rs.Fields(x).Value + "</td>"" + vbcrlf)")
```

NONE

```
txtstream.WriteLine("Response.Write(""<td style=""font-family:Calibri, Sans-Serif;font-size: 12px;color:navy;"" align='left' nowrap='nowrap'>" + rs.Fields(x).Value + "</td>"" + vbcrlf)")
```

Button

```
txtstream.WriteLine("Response.Write(""<td style=""font-family:Calibri, Sans-Serif;font-size: 12px;color:navy;"" align='left' nowrap='true'><button style='width:100%;' value ='" + rs.Fields(x).Value + "'>" + rs.Fields(x).Value + "</button></td>"" + vbcrlf)")
```

Combobox

```
txtstream.WriteLine("Response.Write(""<td style=""font-family:Calibri, Sans-Serif;font-size: 12px;color:navy;"" align='left' nowrap='true'><select><option value = """" + rs.Fields(x).Value + """">" + rs.Fields(x).Value + "</option></select></td>"" + vbcrlf)")
```

Div

```
txtstream.WriteLine("Response.Write(""<td style=""font-family:Calibri, Sans-Serif;font-size: 12px;color:navy;"" align='left' nowrap='true'><div>" + rs.Fields(x).Value + "</div></td>"" + vbcrlf)")
```

Link

```
txtstream.WriteLine("Response.Write(""<td style=""font-family:Calibri, Sans-Serif;font-size: 12px;color:navy;"" align='left' nowrap='true'><a href='" + rs.Fields(x).Value + "'>" + rs.Fields(x).Value + "</a></td>"" + vbcrlf)")
```

Listbox

```
txtstream.WriteLine("Response.Write(""<td style=""font-family:Calibri, Sans-Serif;font-size: 12px;color:navy;"" align='left' nowrap='true'><select multiple><option value = """" + rs.Fields(x).Value + """">" + rs.Fields(x).Value + "</option></select></td>"" + vbcrlf)")
```

Span

```
txtstream.WriteLine("Response.Write(""<td style=""font-family:Calibri, Sans-Serif;font-size: 12px;color:navy;"" align='left' nowrap='true'><span>" + rs.Fields(x).Value + "</span></td>"" + vbcrlf)")
```

Textarea

```
txtstream.WriteLine("Response.Write(""<td style=""font-family:Calibri, Sans-Serif;font-size: 12px;color:navy;"" align='left' nowrap='true'><textarea>" + rs.Fields(x).Value + "</textarea></td>"" + vbcrlf)")
```

Textbox

```
        txtstream.WriteLine("Response.Write(""<td style=""font-family:Calibri, Sans-Serif;font-size: 12px;color:navy;"" align='left' nowrap='true'><input type=text value="""" + rs.Fields(x).Value + """"></input></td>"" + vbcrlf)")
        rs.MoveNext

      txtstream.WriteLine("Response.Write(""</tr>"" + vbcrlf)")

  txtstream.WriteLine("%>")
  txtstream.WriteLine("</table>")
  txtstream.WriteLine("</body>")
```

```
txtstream.WriteLine("</html>")
txtstream.Close()
```

ASPX CODE

BELOW ARE EXAMPLES OF USING ADO THROUGH VBSCRIPT TO CREATE ASPX FILES.

```
Dim ws As Object = CreateObject("WScript.Shell")
Dim fso As Object = CreateObject("Scripting.FileSystemObject")
Dim txtstream As Object =fso.OpenTextFile(ws.CurrentDirectory + "\Products.asp", 2, true, -2)
txtstream.WriteLine("<html>")
txtstream.WriteLine("<head>")
txtstream.WriteLine("<title>" + Tablename + "</title>")
#Add Stylesheet here
txtstream.WriteLine("<body>")
txtstream.WriteLine("</br>")
```

Horizontal Reports

```
txtstream.WriteLine("<table border=0 cellspacing=3 cellpadding=3>")
txtstream.WriteLine("<%")
txtstream.WriteLine("Response.Write(""<tr>"" + vbcrlf)")
For x = 0 to rs.Fields.Count-1
   txtstream.WriteLine("Response.Write(""<th style="" font-family:Calibri, Sans-Serif;font-size: 12px;color:darkred;"" align='left' nowrap='nowrap'>" + rs.Fields(x).Name + "</th>"" + vbcrlf)")
Next
```

```
txtstream.WriteLine("Response.Write(""</tr>"" + vbcrlf)")
Do While(rs.EOF = false)
   txtstream.WriteLine("Response.Write(""<tr>"" + vbcrlf)")
   For x = 0 to rs.Fields.Count-1
```

NONE

```
txtstream.WriteLine("Response.Write(""<td style=""font-family:Calibri, Sans-Serif;font-size: 12px;color:navy;"" align='left' nowrap='nowrap'>" + rs.Fields(x).Value + "</td>"" + vbcrlf)")
```

Button

```
txtstream.WriteLine("Response.Write(""<td style=""font-family:Calibri, Sans-Serif;font-size: 12px;color:navy;"" align='left' nowrap='true'><button style='width:100%;' value ='" + rs.Fields(x).Value + "'>" + rs.Fields(x).Value + "</button></td>"" + vbcrlf)")
```

COMBOBOX

```
txtstream.WriteLine("Response.Write(""<td style=""font-family:Calibri, Sans-Serif;font-size: 12px;color:navy;"" align='left' nowrap='true'><select><option value = """" + rs.Fields(x).Value + """">" + rs.Fields(x).Value + "</option></select></td>"" + vbcrlf)")
```

DIV

```
txtstream.WriteLine("Response.Write(""<td style=""font-family:Calibri, Sans-Serif;font-size: 12px;color:navy;"" align='left' nowrap='true'><div>" + rs.Fields(x).Value + "</div></td>"" + vbcrlf)")
```

LINK

```
txtstream.WriteLine("Response.Write(""<td style=""font-family:Calibri, Sans-Serif;font-size: 12px;color:navy;"" align='left' nowrap='true'><a href='" + rs.Fields(x).Value + "'>" + rs.Fields(x).Value + "</a></td>"" + vbcrlf)")
```

LISTBOX

```
txtstream.WriteLine("Response.Write(""<td style=""font-family:Calibri, Sans-Serif;font-size: 12px;color:navy;"" align='left' nowrap='true'><select multiple><option value = """" + rs.Fields(x).Value + """">" + rs.Fields(x).Value + "</option></select></td>"" + vbcrlf)")
```

SPAN

```
txtstream.WriteLine("Response.Write(""<td style=""font-family:Calibri, Sans-Serif;font-size: 12px;color:navy;"" align='left' nowrap='true'><span>" + rs.Fields(x).Value + "</span></td>"" + vbcrlf)")
```

TEXTAREA

```
txtstream.WriteLine("Response.Write(""<td style=""font-family:Calibri, Sans-Serif;font-size: 12px;color:navy;"" align='left' nowrap='true'><textarea>" + rs.Fields(x).Value + "</textarea></td>"" + vbcrlf)")
```

TEXTBOX

```
txtstream.WriteLine("Response.Write(""<td style=""font-family:Calibri, Sans-Serif;font-size: 12px;color:navy;"" align='left' nowrap='true'><input type=text value="""" + rs.Fields(x).Value + """"></input></td>"" + vbcrlf)")
```

```
        Next
        txtstream.WriteLine("Response.Write(""</tr>"" + vbcrlf)")
        rs.MoveNext
    Loop
    txtstream.WriteLine("%>")
    txtstream.WriteLine("</table>")
    txtstream.WriteLine("</body>")
    txtstream.WriteLine("</html>")
    txtstream.Close()
```

Vertical Reports

```
txtstream.WriteLine("<table border=0 cellspacing=3 cellpadding=3>")
txtstream.WriteLine("<%")
For x = 0 to rs.Fields.Count-1
    txtstream.WriteLine("Response.Write(""<tr><th style="" font-family:Calibri, Sans-Serif;font-size: 12px;color:darkred;"" align='left' nowrap='nowrap'>" + rs.Fields(x).Name + "</th>"" + vbcrlf)")
    rs.MoveFirst()
    Do While(rs.EOF = false)
    txtstream.WriteLine("Response.Write(""<td style=""font-family:Calibri, Sans-Serif;font-size: 12px;color:navy;"">" + rs.Fields(x).Value + "</td>"" + vbcrlf)")
```

NONE

```
txtstream.WriteLine("Response.Write(""<td style=""font-family:Calibri, Sans-Serif;font-size: 12px;color:navy;"" align='left' nowrap='nowrap'>" + rs.Fields(x).Value + "</td>"" + vbcrlf)")
```

Button

```
txtstream.WriteLine("Response.Write(""<td style=""font-family:Calibri, Sans-Serif;font-size: 12px;color:navy;"" align='left' nowrap='true'><button style='width:100%;' value ='" + rs.Fields(x).Value + "'>" + rs.Fields(x).Value + "</button></td>"" + vbcrlf)")
```

Combobox

```
txtstream.WriteLine("Response.Write(""<td style=""font-family:Calibri, Sans-Serif;font-size: 12px;color:navy;"" align='left' nowrap='true'><select><option value = """" + rs.Fields(x).Value + """">" + rs.Fields(x).Value + "</option></select></td>"" + vbcrlf)")
```

Div

```
txtstream.WriteLine("Response.Write(""<td style=""font-family:Calibri, Sans-Serif;font-size: 12px;color:navy;"" align='left' nowrap='true'><div>" + rs.Fields(x).Value + "</div></td>"" + vbcrlf)")
```

Link

```
txtstream.WriteLine("Response.Write(""<td style=""font-family:Calibri, Sans-Serif;font-size: 12px;color:navy;"" align='left' nowrap='true'><a href='" + rs.Fields(x).Value + "'>" + rs.Fields(x).Value + "</a></td>"" + vbcrlf)")
```

Listbox

```
txtstream.WriteLine("Response.Write(""<td style=""font-family:Calibri, Sans-Serif;font-size: 12px;color:navy;"" align='left' nowrap='true'><select multiple><option value = """" + rs.Fields(x).Value + """">" + rs.Fields(x).Value + "</option></select></td>"" + vbcrlf)")
```

Span

```
txtstream.WriteLine("Response.Write(""<td style=""font-family:Calibri, Sans-Serif;font-size: 12px;color:navy;"" align='left' nowrap='true'><span>" + rs.Fields(x).Value + "</span></td>"" + vbcrlf)")
```

Textarea

```
txtstream.WriteLine("Response.Write(""<td style=""font-family:Calibri, Sans-Serif;font-size: 12px;color:navy;"" align='left' nowrap='true'><textarea>" + rs.Fields(x).Value + "</textarea></td>"" + vbcrlf)")
```

Textbox

```
        txtstream.WriteLine("Response.Write(""<td style=""font-family:Calibri, Sans-Serif;font-size: 12px;color:navy;"" align='left' nowrap='true'><input type=text value="""" + rs.Fields(x).Value + """"></input></td>"" + vbcrlf)")
        rs.MoveNext
       Loop
     txtstream.WriteLine("Response.Write(""</tr>"" + vbcrlf)")
Next
txtstream.WriteLine("%>")
txtstream.WriteLine("</table>")
txtstream.WriteLine("</body>")
txtstream.WriteLine("</html>")
```

```
txtstream.Close()
```

Horizontal Tables

```
txtstream.WriteLine("<table style='border:Double;border-width:1px;border-color:navy;' rules=all frames=both cellpadding=2 cellspacing=2 Width=0>")
txtstream.WriteLine("<%")
txtstream.WriteLine("Response.Write(""<tr>"" + vbcrlf)")
For x = 0 to rs.Fields.Count-1
   txtstream.WriteLine("Response.Write(""<th style="" font-family:Calibri, Sans-Serif;font-size: 12px;color:darkred;"" align='left' nowrap='nowrap'>" + rs.Fields(x).Name + "</th>"" + vbcrlf)")
Next
txtstream.WriteLine("Response.Write(""</tr>"" + vbcrlf)")
Do While(rs.EOF = false)
   txtstream.WriteLine("Response.Write(""<tr>"" + vbcrlf)")
      For x = 0 to rs.Fields.Count-1
```

NONE

```
txtstream.WriteLine("Response.Write(""<td style=""font-family:Calibri, Sans-Serif;font-size: 12px;color:navy;"" align='left' nowrap='nowrap'>" + rs.Fields(x).Value + "</td>"" + vbcrlf)")
```

Button

```
txtstream.WriteLine("Response.Write(""<td style=""font-family:Calibri, Sans-Serif;font-size: 12px;color:navy;"" align='left' nowrap='true'><button style='width:100%;' value ='" + rs.Fields(x).Value + "'>" + rs.Fields(x).Value + "</button></td>"" + vbcrlf)")
```

COMBOBOX

```
txtstream.WriteLine("Response.Write(""<td style=""font-family:Calibri, Sans-Serif;font-size: 12px;color:navy;"" align='left' nowrap='true'><select><option
```

```
value = """" + rs.Fields(x).Value + """">" + rs.Fields(x).Value + "</option></select></td>"" + vbcrlf)")
```

DIV

```
txtstream.WriteLine("Response.Write(""<td style=""font-family:Calibri, Sans-Serif;font-size: 12px;color:navy;"" align='left' nowrap='true'><div>" + rs.Fields(x).Value + "</div></td>"" + vbcrlf)")
```

LINK

```
txtstream.WriteLine("Response.Write(""<td style=""font-family:Calibri, Sans-Serif;font-size: 12px;color:navy;"" align='left' nowrap='true'><a href='" + rs.Fields(x).Value + "'>" + rs.Fields(x).Value + "</a></td>"" + vbcrlf)")
```

LISTBOX

```
txtstream.WriteLine("Response.Write(""<td style=""font-family:Calibri, Sans-Serif;font-size: 12px;color:navy;"" align='left' nowrap='true'><select multiple><option value = """" + rs.Fields(x).Value + """">" + rs.Fields(x).Value + "</option></select></td>"" + vbcrlf)")
```

SPAN

```
txtstream.WriteLine("Response.Write(""<td style=""font-family:Calibri, Sans-Serif;font-size: 12px;color:navy;"" align='left' nowrap='true'><span>" + rs.Fields(x).Value + "</span></td>"" + vbcrlf)")
```

TEXTAREA

```
txtstream.WriteLine("Response.Write(""<td style=""font-family:Calibri, Sans-Serif;font-size: 12px;color:navy;"" align='left' nowrap='true'><textarea>" + rs.Fields(x).Value + "</textarea></td>"" + vbcrlf)")
```

TEXTBOX

```
txtstream.WriteLine("Response.Write(""<td style=""font-family:Calibri, Sans-Serif;font-size: 12px;color:navy;"" align='left' nowrap='true'><input type=text value="""" + rs.Fields(x).Value + """"></input></td>"" + vbcrlf)")
Next
```

```
        txtstream.WriteLine("Response.Write(""</tr>"" + vbcrlf)")
        rs.MoveNext
    Loop
    txtstream.WriteLine("%>")
    txtstream.WriteLine("</table>")
    txtstream.WriteLine("</body>")
    txtstream.WriteLine("</html>")
    txtstream.Close()
```

Vertical Tables

```
    txtstream.WriteLine("<table style='border:Double;border-width:1px;border-color:navy;' rules=all frames=both cellpadding=2 cellspacing=2 Width=0>")
    txtstream.WriteLine("<%")
    For x = 0 to rs.Fields.Count-1
        txtstream.WriteLine("Response.Write(""<tr><th style="" font-family:Calibri, Sans-Serif;font-size: 12px;color:darkred;"" align='left' nowrap='nowrap'>" + rs.Fields(x).Name + "</th>"" + vbcrlf)")
        rs.MoveFirst()
        Do While rs.EOF = false
         txtstream.WriteLine("Response.Write(""<td style=""font-family:Calibri, Sans-Serif;font-size: 12px;color:navy;"">" + rs.Fields(x).Value + "</td>"" + vbcrlf)")
```

NONE

```
            txtstream.WriteLine("Response.Write(""<td style=""font-family:Calibri, Sans-Serif;font-size: 12px;color:navy;"" align='left' nowrap='nowrap'>" + rs.Fields(x).Value + "</td>"" + vbcrlf)")
```

Button

```
         txtstream.WriteLine("Response.Write(""<td style=""font-family:Calibri, Sans-Serif;font-size: 12px;color:navy;"" align='left' nowrap='true'><button style='width:100%;' value ='" + rs.Fields(x).Value + "'>" + rs.Fields(x).Value + "</button></td>"" + vbcrlf)")
```

Combobox

```
txtstream.WriteLine("Response.Write(""<td style=""font-family:Calibri, Sans-Serif;font-size: 12px;color:navy;"" align='left' nowrap='true'><select><option value = """" + rs.Fields(x).Value + """">" + rs.Fields(x).Value + "</option></select></td>"" + vbcrlf)")
```

Div

```
txtstream.WriteLine("Response.Write(""<td style=""font-family:Calibri, Sans-Serif;font-size: 12px;color:navy;"" align='left' nowrap='true'><div>" + rs.Fields(x).Value + "</div></td>"" + vbcrlf)")
```

Link

```
txtstream.WriteLine("Response.Write(""<td style=""font-family:Calibri, Sans-Serif;font-size: 12px;color:navy;"" align='left' nowrap='true'><a href='" + rs.Fields(x).Value + "'>" + rs.Fields(x).Value + "</a></td>"" + vbcrlf)")
```

Listbox

```
txtstream.WriteLine("Response.Write(""<td style=""font-family:Calibri, Sans-Serif;font-size: 12px;color:navy;"" align='left' nowrap='true'><select multiple><option value = """" + rs.Fields(x).Value + """">" + rs.Fields(x).Value + "</option></select></td>"" + vbcrlf)")
```

Span

```
txtstream.WriteLine("Response.Write(""<td style=""font-family:Calibri, Sans-Serif;font-size: 12px;color:navy;"" align='left' nowrap='true'><span>" + rs.Fields(x).Value + "</span></td>"" + vbcrlf)")
```

Textarea

```
txtstream.WriteLine("Response.Write(""<td style=""font-family:Calibri, Sans-Serif;font-size: 12px;color:navy;"" align='left' nowrap='true'><textarea>" + rs.Fields(x).Value + "</textarea></td>"" + vbcrlf)")
```

Textbox

```
            txtstream.WriteLine("Response.Write(""<td style=""font-family:Calibri, Sans-Serif;font-size: 12px;color:navy;"" align='left' nowrap='true'><input type=text value=""" + rs.Fields(x).Value + """></input></td>"" + vbcrlf)")
            rs.MoveNext
        loop
        txtstream.WriteLine("Response.Write(""</tr>"" + vbcrlf)")
    next
    txtstream.WriteLine("%>")
    txtstream.WriteLine("</table>")
    txtstream.WriteLine("</body>")
    txtstream.WriteLine("</html>")
    txtstream.Close()
```

HTA CODE

LIKE ASP AND ASPX, HTA BEEN AROUND FOR SOME TIME NOW. Despite the fact the concept appears to be old or outdated You should know that it is still being used as HTML as an EXE.

```
Dim ws As Object = CreateObject("WScript.Shell")
Dim fso As Object = CreateObject("Scripting.FileSystemObject")
Dim txtstream As Object =fso.OpenTextFile(ws.CurrentDirectory + "\Products.hta", 2, true, -2)
txtstream.WriteLine("<html>")
txtstream.WriteLine("<head>")
txtstream.WriteLine("<HTA:APPLICATION ")
txtstream.WriteLine("ID = ""Products"" ")
txtstream.WriteLine("APPLICATIONNAME = ""Products"" ")
txtstream.WriteLine("SCROLL = ""yes"" ")
txtstream.WriteLine("SINGLEINSTANCE = ""yes"" ")
txtstream.WriteLine("WINDOWSTATE = ""maximize"" >")
txtstream.WriteLine("<title>" + Tablename + "</title>")
#Add Stylesheet here
txtstream.WriteLine("<body>")
txtstream.WriteLine("</br>")
```

Horizontal Reports

```
txtstream.WriteLine("<table border=0 cellspacing=3 cellpadding=3>")
txtstream.WriteLine("<tr>")
```

```
For x = 0 to rs.Fields.Count-1
  txtstream.WriteLine("<th style="" font-family:Calibri, Sans-Serif;font-size: 12px;color:darkred;"" align='left' nowrap='nowrap'>" + rs.Fields(x).Name + "</th>")
Next
txtstream.WriteLine("</tr>")
Do While(rs.EOF = false)
  txtstream.WriteLine("<tr>")
  For x = 0 to rs.Fields.Count-1
```

NONE

```
      txtstream.WriteLine("<td style=""font-family:Calibri, Sans-Serif;font-size: 12px;color:navy;"" align='left' nowrap='nowrap'>" + rs.Fields(x).Value + "</td>")
```

Button

```
      txtstream.WriteLine("<td style=""font-family:Calibri, Sans-Serif;font-size: 12px;color:navy;"" align='left' nowrap='true'><button style='width:100%;' value ='" + rs.Fields(x).Value + "'>" + rs.Fields(x).Value + "</button></td>")
```

COMBOBOX

```
      txtstream.WriteLine("<td style=""font-family:Calibri, Sans-Serif;font-size: 12px;color:navy;"" align='left' nowrap='true'><select><option value = """ + rs.Fields(x).Value + """>" + rs.Fields(x).Value + "</option></select></td>")
```

DIV

```
      txtstream.WriteLine("<td style=""font-family:Calibri, Sans-Serif;font-size: 12px;color:navy;"" align='left' nowrap='true'><div>" + rs.Fields(x).Value + "</div></td>")
```

LINK

```
txtstream.WriteLine("<td style=""font-family:Calibri, Sans-Serif;font-size: 12px;color:navy;"" align='left' nowrap='true'><a href='" + rs.Fields(x).Value + "'>" + rs.Fields(x).Value + "</a></td>")
```

LISTBOX

```
txtstream.WriteLine("<td style=""font-family:Calibri, Sans-Serif;font-size: 12px;color:navy;"" align='left' nowrap='true'><select multiple><option value = """" + rs.Fields(x).Value + """">" + rs.Fields(x).Value + "</option></select></td>")
```

SPAN

```
txtstream.WriteLine("<td style=""font-family:Calibri, Sans-Serif;font-size: 12px;color:navy;"" align='left' nowrap='true'><span>" + rs.Fields(x).Value + "</span></td>")
```

TEXTAREA

```
txtstream.WriteLine("<td style=""font-family:Calibri, Sans-Serif;font-size: 12px;color:navy;"" align='left' nowrap='true'><textarea>" + rs.Fields(x).Value + "</textarea></td>")
```

TEXTBOX

```
txtstream.WriteLine("<td style=""font-family:Calibri, Sans-Serif;font-size: 12px;color:navy;"" align='left' nowrap='true'><input type=text value="""" + rs.Fields(x).Value + """"></input></td>")
        Next
        txtstream.WriteLine("</tr>")
        rs.MoveNext
    Loop
    txtstream.WriteLine("</table>")
    txtstream.WriteLine("</body>")
    txtstream.WriteLine("</html>")
    txtstream.Close()
```

```
txtstream.WriteLine("<table border=0 cellspacing=3 cellpadding=3>")
For x = 0 to rs.Fields.Count-1
    txtstream.WriteLine("<tr><th style="" font-family:Calibri, Sans-Serif;font-size: 12px;color:darkred;"" align='left' nowrap='nowrap'>" + rs.Fields(x).Name + "</th>")
    rs.MoveFirst()
    Do While(rs.EOF = false)
    txtstream.WriteLine("<td style=""font-family:Calibri, Sans-Serif;font-size: 12px;color:navy;"">" + rs.Fields(x).Value + "</td>")
```

NONE

```
txtstream.WriteLine("<td style=""font-family:Calibri, Sans-Serif;font-size: 12px;color:navy;"" align='left' nowrap='nowrap'>" + rs.Fields(x).Value + "</td>")
```

Button

```
txtstream.WriteLine("<td style=""font-family:Calibri, Sans-Serif;font-size: 12px;color:navy;"" align='left' nowrap='true'><button style='width:100%;' value ='" + rs.Fields(x).Value + "'>" + rs.Fields(x).Value + "</button></td>")
```

Combobox

```
txtstream.WriteLine("<td style=""font-family:Calibri, Sans-Serif;font-size: 12px;color:navy;"" align='left' nowrap='true'><select><option value = """ + rs.Fields(x).Value + """>" + rs.Fields(x).Value + "</option></select></td>")
```

Div

```
txtstream.WriteLine("<td style=""font-family:Calibri, Sans-Serif;font-size: 12px;color:navy;"" align='left' nowrap='true'><div>" + rs.Fields(x).Value + "</div></td>")
```

Link

```
txtstream.WriteLine("<td style=""font-family:Calibri, Sans-Serif;font-size: 12px;color:navy;"" align='left' nowrap='true'><a href='" + rs.Fields(x).Value + "'>" + rs.Fields(x).Value + "</a></td>")
```

Listbox

```
txtstream.WriteLine("<td style=""font-family:Calibri, Sans-Serif;font-size: 12px;color:navy;"" align='left' nowrap='true'><select multiple><option value = """ + rs.Fields(x).Value + """>" + rs.Fields(x).Value + "</option></select></td>")
```

Span

```
txtstream.WriteLine("<td style=""font-family:Calibri, Sans-Serif;font-size: 12px;color:navy;"" align='left' nowrap='true'><span>" + rs.Fields(x).Value + "</span></td>")
```

Textarea

```
txtstream.WriteLine("<td style=""font-family:Calibri, Sans-Serif;font-size: 12px;color:navy;"" align='left' nowrap='true'><textarea>" + rs.Fields(x).Value + "</textarea></td>")
```

Textbox

```
txtstream.WriteLine("<td style=""font-family:Calibri, Sans-Serif;font-size: 12px;color:navy;"" align='left' nowrap='true'><input type=text value=""" + rs.Fields(x).Value + """></input></td>")
        rs.MoveNext
      Loop
    txtstream.WriteLine("</tr>")
Next
txtstream.WriteLine("</table>")
txtstream.WriteLine("</body>")
txtstream.WriteLine("</html>")
txtstream.Close()
```

Horizontal Tables

```
txtstream.WriteLine("<table style='border:Double;border-width:1px;border-color:navy;' rules=all frames=both cellpadding=2 cellspacing=2 Width=0>")
txtstream.WriteLine("<tr>")
For x = 0 to rs.Fields.Count-1
  txtstream.WriteLine("<th style="" font-family:Calibri, Sans-Serif;font-size: 12px;color:darkred;"" align='left' nowrap='nowrap'>" + rs.Fields(x).Name + "</th>")
Next
txtstream.WriteLine("</tr>")
Do While(rs.EOF = false)
  txtstream.WriteLine("<tr>")
    For x = 0 to rs.Fields.Count-1
```

NONE

```
txtstream.WriteLine("<td style=""font-family:Calibri, Sans-Serif;font-size: 12px;color:navy;"" align='left' nowrap='nowrap'>" + rs.Fields(x).Value + "</td>")
```

Button

```
txtstream.WriteLine("<td style=""font-family:Calibri, Sans-Serif;font-size: 12px;color:navy;"" align='left' nowrap='true'><button style='width:100%;' value ='" + rs.Fields(x).Value + "'>" + rs.Fields(x).Value + "</button></td>")
```

COMBOBOX

```
txtstream.WriteLine("<td style=""font-family:Calibri, Sans-Serif;font-size: 12px;color:navy;"" align='left' nowrap='true'><select><option value = """ + rs.Fields(x).Value + """>" + rs.Fields(x).Value + "</option></select></td>")
```

DIV

```
txtstream.WriteLine("<td style=""font-family:Calibri, Sans-Serif;font-size: 12px;color:navy;"" align='left' nowrap='true'><div>" + rs.Fields(x).Value + "</div></td>")
```

LINK

```
txtstream.WriteLine("<td style=""font-family:Calibri, Sans-Serif;font-size: 12px;color:navy;"" align='left' nowrap='true'><a href='" + rs.Fields(x).Value + "'>" + rs.Fields(x).Value + "</a></td>")
```

LISTBOX

```
txtstream.WriteLine("<td style=""font-family:Calibri, Sans-Serif;font-size: 12px;color:navy;"" align='left' nowrap='true'><select multiple><option value = """" + rs.Fields(x).Value + """">" + rs.Fields(x).Value + "</option></select></td>")
```

SPAN

```
txtstream.WriteLine("<td style=""font-family:Calibri, Sans-Serif;font-size: 12px;color:navy;"" align='left' nowrap='true'><span>" + rs.Fields(x).Value + "</span></td>")
```

TEXTAREA

```
txtstream.WriteLine("<td style=""font-family:Calibri, Sans-Serif;font-size: 12px;color:navy;"" align='left' nowrap='true'><textarea>" + rs.Fields(x).Value + "</textarea></td>")
```

TEXTBOX

```
            txtstream.WriteLine("<td style=""font-family:Calibri, Sans-Serif;font-size: 12px;color:navy;"" align='left' nowrap='true'><input type=text value="""" + rs.Fields(x).Value + """"></input></td>")
        Next
        txtstream.WriteLine("</tr>")
        rs.MoveNext
    Loop
    txtstream.WriteLine("</table>")
    txtstream.WriteLine("</body>")
```

```
txtstream.WriteLine("</html>")
txtstream.Close()
```

Vertical Tables

```
txtstream.WriteLine("<table style='border:Double;border-width:1px;border-color:navy;' rules=all frames=both cellpadding=2 cellspacing=2 Width=0>")
For x = 0 to rs.Fields.Count-1
    txtstream.WriteLine("<tr><th style="" font-family:Calibri, Sans-Serif;font-size: 12px;color:darkred;"" align='left' nowrap='nowrap'>" + rs.Fields(x).Name + "</th>")
    rs.MoveFirst()
    Do While rs.EOF = false
     txtstream.WriteLine("<td style=""font-family:Calibri, Sans-Serif;font-size: 12px;color:navy;"">" + rs.Fields(x).Value + "</td>")
```

NONE

```
txtstream.WriteLine("<td style=""font-family:Calibri, Sans-Serif;font-size: 12px;color:navy;"" align='left' nowrap='nowrap'>" + rs.Fields(x).Value + "</td>")
```

Button

```
txtstream.WriteLine("<td style=""font-family:Calibri, Sans-Serif;font-size: 12px;color:navy;"" align='left' nowrap='true'><button style='width:100%;' value ='" + rs.Fields(x).Value + "'>" + rs.Fields(x).Value + "</button></td>")
```

Combobox

```
txtstream.WriteLine("<td style=""font-family:Calibri, Sans-Serif;font-size: 12px;color:navy;"" align='left' nowrap='true'><select><option value = """ + rs.Fields(x).Value + """>" + rs.Fields(x).Value + "</option></select></td>")
```

Div

```
txtstream.WriteLine("<td style=""font-family:Calibri, Sans-Serif;font-size: 12px;color:navy;"" align='left' nowrap='true'><div>" + rs.Fields(x).Value + "</div></td>")
```

Link

```
txtstream.WriteLine("<td style=""font-family:Calibri, Sans-Serif;font-size: 12px;color:navy;"" align='left' nowrap='true'><a href='" + rs.Fields(x).Value + "'>" + rs.Fields(x).Value + "</a></td>")
```

Listbox

```
txtstream.WriteLine("<td style=""font-family:Calibri, Sans-Serif;font-size: 12px;color:navy;"" align='left' nowrap='true'><select multiple><option value = """ + rs.Fields(x).Value + """>" + rs.Fields(x).Value + "</option></select></td>")
```

Span

```
txtstream.WriteLine("<td style=""font-family:Calibri, Sans-Serif;font-size: 12px;color:navy;"" align='left' nowrap='true'><span>" + rs.Fields(x).Value + "</span></td>")
```

Textarea

```
txtstream.WriteLine("<td style=""font-family:Calibri, Sans-Serif;font-size: 12px;color:navy;"" align='left' nowrap='true'><textarea>" + rs.Fields(x).Value + "</textarea></td>")
```

Textbox

```
            txtstream.WriteLine("<td style=""font-family:Calibri, Sans-Serif;font-size: 12px;color:navy;"" align='left' nowrap='true'><input type=text value=""" + rs.Fields(x).Value + """></input></td>")
            rs.MoveNext
        Loop
        txtstream.WriteLine("</tr>")
    Next
    txtstream.WriteLine("</table>")
```

```
txtstream.WriteLine("</body>")
txtstream.WriteLine("</html>")
txtstream.Close()
```

HTML CODE

WHAT CAN I SAY ABOUT HTML5 AND CSS THAT HASN'T BEEN SAID ALREADY? Well, I can say that it has come a long way since the 1990s.

```
Dim ws As Object = CreateObject("WScript.Shell")
Dim fso As Object = CreateObject("Scripting.FileSystemObject")
Dim txtstream As Object =fso.OpenTextFile(ws.CurrentDirectory + "\Products.html", 2, true, -2)
txtstream.WriteLine("<html>")
txtstream.WriteLine("<head>")
txtstream.WriteLine("<title>" + Tablename + "</title>")
#Add Stylesheet here
txtstream.WriteLine("<body>")
txtstream.WriteLine("</br>")
```

Horizontal Reports

```
txtstream.WriteLine("<table border=0 cellspacing=3 cellpadding=3>")
txtstream.WriteLine("<tr>")
For x = 0 to rs.Fields.Count-1
```

```
txtstream.WriteLine("<th style="" font-family:Calibri, Sans-Serif;font-size: 12px;color:darkred;"" align='left' nowrap='nowrap'>" + rs.Fields(x).Name + "</th>")

    txtstream.WriteLine("</tr>")
    Next
    Do While(rs.EOF = false)
      txtstream.WriteLine("<tr>")
      For x = 0 to rs.Fields.Count-1
```

NONE

```
txtstream.WriteLine("<td style=""font-family:Calibri, Sans-Serif;font-size: 12px;color:navy;"" align='left' nowrap='nowrap'>" + rs.Fields(x).Value + "</td>")
```

Button

```
txtstream.WriteLine("<td style=""font-family:Calibri, Sans-Serif;font-size: 12px;color:navy;"" align='left' nowrap='true'><button style='width:100%;' value ='" + rs.Fields(x).Value + "'>" + rs.Fields(x).Value + "</button></td>")
```

COMBOBOX

```
txtstream.WriteLine("<td style=""font-family:Calibri, Sans-Serif;font-size: 12px;color:navy;"" align='left' nowrap='true'><select><option value = """ + rs.Fields(x).Value + """>" + rs.Fields(x).Value + "</option></select></td>")
```

DIV

```
txtstream.WriteLine("<td style=""font-family:Calibri, Sans-Serif;font-size: 12px;color:navy;"" align='left' nowrap='true'><div>" + rs.Fields(x).Value + "</div></td>")
```

LINK

```
txtstream.WriteLine("<td style=""font-family:Calibri, Sans-Serif;font-size: 12px;color:navy;"" align='left' nowrap='true'><a href='" + rs.Fields(x).Value + "'>" + rs.Fields(x).Value + "</a></td>")
```

LISTBOX

```
txtstream.WriteLine("<td style=""font-family:Calibri, Sans-Serif;font-size: 12px;color:navy;"" align='left' nowrap='true'><select multiple><option value = """" + rs.Fields(x).Value + """">" + rs.Fields(x).Value + "</option></select></td>")
```

SPAN

```
txtstream.WriteLine("<td style=""font-family:Calibri, Sans-Serif;font-size: 12px;color:navy;"" align='left' nowrap='true'><span>" + rs.Fields(x).Value + "</span></td>")
```

TEXTAREA

```
txtstream.WriteLine("<td style=""font-family:Calibri, Sans-Serif;font-size: 12px;color:navy;"" align='left' nowrap='true'><textarea>" + rs.Fields(x).Value + "</textarea></td>")
```

TEXTBOX

```
        txtstream.WriteLine("<td style=""font-family:Calibri, Sans-Serif;font-size: 12px;color:navy;"" align='left' nowrap='true'><input type=text value="""" + rs.Fields(x).Value + """"></input></td>")
        Next
        txtstream.WriteLine("</tr>")
        rs.MoveNext
    Loop
    txtstream.WriteLine("</table>")
    txtstream.WriteLine("</body>")
    txtstream.WriteLine("</html>")
    txtstream.Close()
```

```
txtstream.WriteLine("<table border=0 cellspacing=3 cellpadding=3>")
For x = 0 to rs.Fields.Count-1
    txtstream.WriteLine("<tr><th style="" font-family:Calibri, Sans-Serif;font-size: 12px;color:darkred;"" align='left' nowrap='nowrap'>" + rs.Fields(x).Name + "</th>")
    rs.MoveFirst()
    Do While(rs.EOF = false)
    txtstream.WriteLine("<td style=""font-family:Calibri, Sans-Serif;font-size: 12px;color:navy;"">" + rs.Fields(x).Value + "</td>")
```

NONE

```
txtstream.WriteLine("<td style=""font-family:Calibri, Sans-Serif;font-size: 12px;color:navy;"" align='left' nowrap='nowrap'>" + rs.Fields(x).Value + "</td>")
```

Button

```
txtstream.WriteLine("<td style=""font-family:Calibri, Sans-Serif;font-size: 12px;color:navy;"" align='left' nowrap='true'><button style='width:100%;' value ='" + rs.Fields(x).Value + "'>" + rs.Fields(x).Value + "</button></td>")
```

Combobox

```
txtstream.WriteLine("<td style=""font-family:Calibri, Sans-Serif;font-size: 12px;color:navy;"" align='left' nowrap='true'><select><option value = """ + rs.Fields(x).Value + """>" + rs.Fields(x).Value + "</option></select></td>")
```

Div

```
txtstream.WriteLine("<td style=""font-family:Calibri, Sans-Serif;font-size: 12px;color:navy;"" align='left' nowrap='true'><div>" + rs.Fields(x).Value + "</div></td>")
```

Link

```
txtstream.WriteLine("<td style=""font-family:Calibri, Sans-Serif;font-size: 12px;color:navy;"" align='left' nowrap='true'><a href='" + rs.Fields(x).Value + "'>" + rs.Fields(x).Value + "</a></td>")
```

Listbox

```
txtstream.WriteLine("<td style=""font-family:Calibri, Sans-Serif;font-size: 12px;color:navy;"" align='left' nowrap='true'><select multiple><option value = """ + rs.Fields(x).Value + """>" + rs.Fields(x).Value + "</option></select></td>")
```

Span

```
txtstream.WriteLine("<td style=""font-family:Calibri, Sans-Serif;font-size: 12px;color:navy;"" align='left' nowrap='true'><span>" + rs.Fields(x).Value + "</span></td>")
```

Textarea

```
txtstream.WriteLine("<td style=""font-family:Calibri, Sans-Serif;font-size: 12px;color:navy;"" align='left' nowrap='true'><textarea>" + rs.Fields(x).Value + "</textarea></td>")
```

Textbox

```
        txtstream.WriteLine("<td style=""font-family:Calibri, Sans-Serif;font-size: 12px;color:navy;"" align='left' nowrap='true'><input type=text value=""" + rs.Fields(x).Value + """></input></td>")
        rs.MoveNext
       Loop
     txtstream.WriteLine("</tr>")
Next
txtstream.WriteLine("</table>")
txtstream.WriteLine("</body>")
txtstream.WriteLine("</html>")
txtstream.Close()
```

Horizontal Tables

```
txtstream.WriteLine("<table style='border:Double;border-width:1px;border-color:navy;' rules=all frames=both cellpadding=2 cellspacing=2 Width=0>")
txtstream.WriteLine("<tr>")
For x = 0 to rs.Fields.Count-1
  txtstream.WriteLine("<th style="" font-family:Calibri, Sans-Serif;font-size: 12px;color:darkred;"" align='left' nowrap='nowrap'>" + rs.Fields(x).Name + "</th>")
Next
txtstream.WriteLine("</tr>")
Do While(rs.EOF = false)
  txtstream.WriteLine("<tr>")
    For x = 0 to rs.Fields.Count-1
```

NONE

```
txtstream.WriteLine("<td style=""font-family:Calibri, Sans-Serif;font-size: 12px;color:navy;"" align='left' nowrap='nowrap'>" + rs.Fields(x).Value + "</td>")
```

Button

```
txtstream.WriteLine("<td style=""font-family:Calibri, Sans-Serif;font-size: 12px;color:navy;"" align='left' nowrap='true'><button style='width:100%;' value ='" + rs.Fields(x).Value + "'>" + rs.Fields(x).Value + "</button></td>")
```

COMBOBOX

```
txtstream.WriteLine("<td style=""font-family:Calibri, Sans-Serif;font-size: 12px;color:navy;"" align='left' nowrap='true'><select><option value = """ + rs.Fields(x).Value + """>" + rs.Fields(x).Value + "</option></select></td>")
```

DIV

```
txtstream.WriteLine("<td style=""font-family:Calibri, Sans-Serif;font-size: 12px;color:navy;"" align='left' nowrap='true'><div>" + rs.Fields(x).Value + "</div></td>")
```

LINK

```
txtstream.WriteLine("<td style=""font-family:Calibri, Sans-Serif;font-size: 12px;color:navy;"" align='left' nowrap='true'><a href='" + rs.Fields(x).Value + "'>" + rs.Fields(x).Value + "</a></td>")
```

LISTBOX

```
txtstream.WriteLine("<td style=""font-family:Calibri, Sans-Serif;font-size: 12px;color:navy;"" align='left' nowrap='true'><select multiple><option value = """ + rs.Fields(x).Value + """>" + rs.Fields(x).Value + "</option></select></td>")
```

SPAN

```
txtstream.WriteLine("<td style=""font-family:Calibri, Sans-Serif;font-size: 12px;color:navy;"" align='left' nowrap='true'><span>" + rs.Fields(x).Value + "</span></td>")
```

TEXTAREA

```
txtstream.WriteLine("<td style=""font-family:Calibri, Sans-Serif;font-size: 12px;color:navy;"" align='left' nowrap='true'><textarea>" + rs.Fields(x).Value + "</textarea></td>")
```

TEXTBOX

```
        txtstream.WriteLine("<td style=""font-family:Calibri, Sans-Serif;font-size: 12px;color:navy;"" align='left' nowrap='true'><input type=text value=""" + rs.Fields(x).Value + """></input></td>")
        Next
        txtstream.WriteLine("</tr>")
        rs.MoveNext
    Loop
    txtstream.WriteLine("</table>")
    txtstream.WriteLine("</body>")
    txtstream.WriteLine("</html>")
    txtstream.Close()
```

Vertical Tables

```
txtstream.WriteLine("<table style='border:Double;border-width:1px;border-color:navy;' rules=all frames=both cellpadding=2 cellspacing=2 Width=0>")
For x = 0 to rs.Fields.Count-1
    txtstream.WriteLine("<tr><th style="" font-family:Calibri, Sans-Serif;font-size: 12px;color:darkred;"" align='left' nowrap='nowrap'>" + rs.Fields(x).Name + "</th>")
    rs.MoveFirst()
    Do While rs.EOF = false
     txtstream.WriteLine("<td style=""font-family:Calibri, Sans-Serif;font-size: 12px;color:navy;"">" + rs.Fields(x).Value + "</td>")
```

NONE

```
txtstream.WriteLine("<td style=""font-family:Calibri, Sans-Serif;font-size: 12px;color:navy;"" align='left' nowrap='nowrap'>" + rs.Fields(x).Value + "</td>")
```

Button

```
txtstream.WriteLine("<td style=""font-family:Calibri, Sans-Serif;font-size: 12px;color:navy;"" align='left' nowrap='true'><button style='width:100%;' value ='" + rs.Fields(x).Value + "'>" + rs.Fields(x).Value + "</button></td>")
```

Combobox

```
txtstream.WriteLine("<td style=""font-family:Calibri, Sans-Serif;font-size: 12px;color:navy;"" align='left' nowrap='true'><select><option value = """" + rs.Fields(x).Value + """">" + rs.Fields(x).Value + "</option></select></td>")
```

Div

```
txtstream.WriteLine("<td style=""font-family:Calibri, Sans-Serif;font-size: 12px;color:navy;"" align='left' nowrap='true'><div>" + rs.Fields(x).Value + "</div></td>")
```

Link

```
txtstream.WriteLine("<td style=""font-family:Calibri, Sans-Serif;font-size: 12px;color:navy;"" align='left' nowrap='true'><a href='" + rs.Fields(x).Value + "'>" + rs.Fields(x).Value + "</a></td>")
```

Listbox

```
txtstream.WriteLine("<td style=""font-family:Calibri, Sans-Serif;font-size: 12px;color:navy;"" align='left' nowrap='true'><select multiple><option value = """ + rs.Fields(x).Value + """>" + rs.Fields(x).Value + "</option></select></td>")
```

Span

```
txtstream.WriteLine("<td style=""font-family:Calibri, Sans-Serif;font-size: 12px;color:navy;"" align='left' nowrap='true'><span>" + rs.Fields(x).Value + "</span></td>")
```

Textarea

```
txtstream.WriteLine("<td style=""font-family:Calibri, Sans-Serif;font-size: 12px;color:navy;"" align='left' nowrap='true'><textarea>" + rs.Fields(x).Value + "</textarea></td>")
```

Textbox

```
        txtstream.WriteLine("<td style=""font-family:Calibri, Sans-Serif;font-size: 12px;color:navy;"" align='left' nowrap='true'><input type=text value=""" + rs.Fields(x).Value + """></input></td>")
        rs.MoveNext
        Loop
        txtstream.WriteLine("</tr>")
    Next
    txtstream.WriteLine("</table>")
    txtstream.WriteLine("</body>")
    txtstream.WriteLine("</html>")
    txtstream.Close()
```

DELIMITED FILES

THERE ARE MANY DIFFERENT KINDS OF DELIMITED FILES. The ones we are going to be using are the most common ones. And by Common, this will include:

- Colon Delimited
- Comma Delimited
- Exclamation Delimited
- Semi-Colon Delimited
- Tab Delimited
- Tilde Delimited

Essentially, the only differences in the code is how the delimiter is used, but the code examples are also going to show you how the information can be arranged in both Horizontal and Vertical Views.

COLON DELIMITED HORIZONTAL VIEW

```
Dim ws As Object = CreateObject("WScript.Shell")
Dim fso As Object = CreateObject("Scripting.FileSystemObject")
Dim txtstream As Object =fso.OpenTextFile(ws.CurrentDirectory + "\Products.txt", 2, true, -2)
tstr= ""
For x = 0 to rs.Fields.Count-1
   if tstr <> "" Then
      tstr = tstr + ":"
   End If
   tstr = tstr + rs.Fields(x).Name
Next
txtstream.Writeline(tstr)
tstr = ""
rs.MoveFirst()
Do While(rs.EOF = false)
   For x = 0 to rs.Fields.Count-1
      if tstr <> "" Then
         tstr = tstr + ":"
      End If
      tstr = tstr + chr(34) + rs.Fields(x).Value + chr(34)
   Next
   txtstream.Writeline(tstr)
   tstr = ""
   rs.MoveNext
Loop
```

COLON DELIMITED VERTICAL VIEW

```
For x = 0 to rs.Fields.Count-1
   tstr = rs.Fields(x).Name
   rs.MoveFirst()
   Do While(rs.EOF = false)
      if tstr <> "" Then
         tstr = tstr + ":"
      End If
```

```
        tstr = tstr + chr(34) + rs.Fields(x).Value + chr(34)
        rs.MoveNext
      Loop
      txtstream.Writeline(tstr)
      tstr = ""
    Next
    txtstream.Close
```

COMMA DELIMITED HORIZONTAL

```
    Dim ws As Object =  CreateObject("WScript.Shell")
    Dim fso As Object =  CreateObject("Scripting.FileSystemObject")
    Dim txtstream As Object =fso.OpenTextFile(ws.CurrentDirectory + "\Products.csv", 2, true, -2)
    tstr= ""
    For x = 0 to rs.Fields.Count-1
      if tstr <> "" Then
        tstr = tstr + ","
      End If
      tstr = tstr + rs.Fields(x).Name
    Next
    txtstream.Writeline(tstr)
    tstr = ""
    rs.MoveFirst()
    Do While(rs.EOF = false)
      For x = 0 to rs.Fields.Count-1
        if tstr <> "" Then
          tstr = tstr + ","
        End If
        tstr = tstr + chr(34) + rs.Fields(x).Value + chr(34)
      Next
      txtstream.Writeline(tstr)
      tstr = ""
      rs.MoveNext
    Loop
```

COMMA DELIMITED VERTICAL

```
Dim ws As Object = CreateObject("WScript.Shell")
Dim fso As Object = CreateObject("Scripting.FileSystemObject")
Dim txtstream As Object =fso.OpenTextFile(ws.CurrentDirectory +
"\Products.csv", 2, true, -2)

For x = 0 to rs.Fields.Count-1
   tstr = rs.Fields(x).Name
   rs.MoveFirst()
   Do While(rs.EOF = false)
      if tstr <> "" Then
         tstr = tstr + ","
      End If
      tstr = tstr + chr(34) + rs.Fields(x).Value + chr(34)
      rs.MoveNext
   Loop
   txtstream.Writeline(tstr)
   tstr = ""
Next
txtstream.Close
```

EXCLAMATION DELIMITED HORIZONTAL

```
Dim ws As Object = CreateObject("WScript.Shell")
Dim fso As Object = CreateObject("Scripting.FileSystemObject")
Dim txtstream As Object =fso.OpenTextFile(ws.CurrentDirectory +
"\Products.txt", 2, true, -2)
tstr= ""
For x = 0 to rs.Fields.Count-1
   if tstr <> "" Then
      tstr = tstr + "!"
   End If
   tstr = tstr + rs.Fields(x).Name
Next
txtstream.Writeline(tstr)
```

```
tstr = ""
rs.MoveFirst()
Do While(rs.EOF = false)
   For x = 0 to rs.Fields.Count-1
      if tstr <> "" Then
         tstr = tstr + "!"
      End If
      tstr = tstr + chr(34) + rs.Fields(x).Value + chr(34)
   Next
   txtstream.Writeline(tstr)
   tstr = ""
   rs.MoveNext
Loop
```

EXCLAMATION DELIMITED VERTICAL

```
Dim ws As Object = CreateObject("WScript.Shell")
Dim fso As Object = CreateObject("Scripting.FileSystemObject")
Dim txtstream As Object =fso.OpenTextFile(ws.CurrentDirectory +
"\Products.txt", 2, true, -2)

For x = 0 to rs.Fields.Count-1
   tstr = rs.Fields(x).Name
   rs.MoveFirst()
   Do While(rs.EOF = false)
      if tstr <> "" Then
         tstr = tstr + "!"
      End If
      tstr = tstr + chr(34) + rs.Fields(x).Value + chr(34)
      rs.MoveNext
   Loop
   txtstream.Writeline(tstr)
   tstr = ""
Next
txtstream.Close
```

SEMI COLON DELIMITED HORIZONTAL

```
Dim ws As Object = CreateObject("WScript.Shell")
Dim fso As Object = CreateObject("Scripting.FileSystemObject")
Dim txtstream As Object =fso.OpenTextFile(ws.CurrentDirectory + "\Products.txt", 2, true, -2)
tstr= ""
For x = 0 to rs.Fields.Count-1
   if tstr <> "" Then
      tstr = tstr + ";"
   End If
   tstr = tstr + rs.Fields(x).Name
Next
txtstream.Writeline(tstr)
tstr = ""
rs.MoveFirst()
Do While(rs.EOF = false)
   For x = 0 to rs.Fields.Count-1
      if tstr <> "" Then
         tstr = tstr + ";"
      End If
      tstr = tstr + chr(34) + rs.Fields(x).Value + chr(34)
   Next
   txtstream.Writeline(tstr)
   tstr = ""
   rs.MoveNext
Loop
```

SEMI COLON DELIMITED VERTICAL

```
Dim ws As Object = CreateObject("WScript.Shell")
Dim fso As Object = CreateObject("Scripting.FileSystemObject")
Dim txtstream As Object =fso.OpenTextFile(ws.CurrentDirectory + "\Products.txt", 2, true, -2)

For x = 0 to rs.Fields.Count-1
   tstr = rs.Fields(x).Name
   rs.MoveFirst()
```

```
    Do While(rs.EOF = false)
      if tstr <> "" Then
        tstr = tstr + ";"
      End If
      tstr = tstr + chr(34) + rs.Fields(x).Value + chr(34)
      rs.MoveNext
    Loop
    txtstream.Writeline(tstr)
    tstr = ""
  Next
  txtstream.Close
```

TAB DELIMITED HORIZONTAL

```
  Dim ws As Object = CreateObject("WScript.Shell")
  Dim fso As Object = CreateObject("Scripting.FileSystemObject")
  Dim txtstream As Object =fso.OpenTextFile(ws.CurrentDirectory + "\Products.txt", 2, true, -2)
  tstr= ""

  For x = 0 to rs.Fields.Count-1
    if tstr <> "" Then
      tstr = tstr + vbTab
    End If
    tstr = tstr + rs.Fields(x).Name
  Next
  txtstream.Writeline(tstr)
  tstr = ""
  rs.MoveFirst()
  Do While(rs.EOF = false)
    For x = 0 to rs.Fields.Count-1
      if tstr <> "" Then
        tstr = tstr + vbTab
      End If
      tstr = tstr + chr(34) + rs.Fields(x).Value + chr(34)
    Next
    txtstream.Writeline(tstr)
    tstr = ""
```

```
    rs.MoveNext
  Loop
```

TAB DELIMITED VERTICAL

```
  Dim ws As Object =  CreateObject("WScript.Shell")
  Dim fso As Object =  CreateObject("Scripting.FileSystemObject")
  Dim    txtstream    As    Object    =fso.OpenTextFile(ws.CurrentDirectory    +
"\Products.txt", 2, true, -2)

  For x = 0 to rs.Fields.Count-1
    tstr = rs.Fields(x).Name
    rs.MoveFirst()
    Do While(rs.EOF = false)
      if tstr <> "" Then
        tstr = tstr + vbTab
      End If
      tstr = tstr + chr(34) + rs.Fields(x).Value + chr(34)
      rs.MoveNext
    Loop
    txtstream.Writeline(tstr)
    tstr = ""
  Next
  txtstream.Close
```

TILDE DELIMITED HORIZONTAL

```
  Dim ws As Object =  CreateObject("WScript.Shell")
  Dim fso As Object =  CreateObject("Scripting.FileSystemObject")
  Dim    txtstream    As    Object    =fso.OpenTextFile(ws.CurrentDirectory    +
"\Products.txt", 2, true, -2)
  tstr= ""
  For x = 0 to rs.Fields.Count-1
    if tstr <> "" Then
      tstr = tstr + "~"
```

```
      End If
      tstr = tstr + rs.Fields(x).Name
   Next
   txtstream.Writeline(tstr)
   tstr = ""
   rs.MoveFirst()
   Do While(rs.EOF = false)
      For x = 0 to rs.Fields.Count-1
         if tstr <> "" Then
            tstr = tstr + "~"
         End If
         tstr = tstr + chr(34) + rs.Fields(x).Value + chr(34)
      Next
      txtstream.Writeline(tstr)
      tstr = ""
      rs.MoveNext
   Loop
```

TILDE DELIMITED VERTICAL

```
   Dim ws As Object =  CreateObject("WScript.Shell")
   Dim fso As Object =  CreateObject("Scripting.FileSystemObject")
   Dim txtstream As Object =fso.OpenTextFile(ws.CurrentDirectory +
"\Products.txt", 2, true, -2)
   For x = 0 to rs.Fields.Count-1
      tstr = rs.Fields(x).Name
      rs.MoveFirst()
      Do While(rs.EOF = false)
         if tstr <> "" Then
            tstr = tstr + "~"
         End If
         tstr = tstr + chr(34) + rs.Fields(x).Value + chr(34)
         rs.MoveNext
      Loop
      txtstream.Writeline(tstr)
      tstr = ""
   Next
   txtstream.Close
```

XML FILES

In this section of the book, we're going to be Coding for the creation of Attribute XML Element XML, Element XML for XSL and Schema XML

ATTRIBUTE XML USING A TEXT FILE

```
ws  = CreateObject("WScript.Shell")
fso  = CreateObject("Scripting.FileSystemObject")
txtstream  = fso.OpenTextFile("C:\Products.xml", 2, true, -2)
txtstream.WriteLine("<?xml version='1.0' encoding='iso-8859-1'?>")
txtstream.WriteLine("<data>")
rs.MoveFirst()
Do While(rs.EOF = false)
   txtstream.WriteLine("<Products>")
   For x in range(rs.Fields.Count):
      txtstream.WriteLine("<property name = """" + rs.Fields(x).Name + """" value="""" + rs.Fields(x).value + """"/>")
   Next
   txtstream.WriteLine("</Products>")
rs.MoveNext()
Loop
txtstream.WriteLine("</data>")
txtstream.Close
```

ATTRIBUTE XML USING THE DOM

```
Dim xmldoc as Object  = CreateObject("MSXML2.DOMDocument")
Dim  pi  As  Object  =  xmldoc.CreateProcessingInstruction("xml",
"version='1.0' encoding='ISO-8859-1'")
Dim oRoot As Object  = xmldoc.CreateElement("data")
xmldoc.AppendChild(pi)
Do While rs.EOF  = false
  Dim oNode As Object  = xmldoc.CreateNode(1, "Products", "")
  for x in range(rs.Fields.Count):
    Dim oNode1 As Object = xmldoc.CreateNode(1, "Property", "")
    Dim oAtt As Object = = xmldoc.CreateAttribute("NAME")
    oAtt.Value = rs.Fields(x).Name
    oNode1.Attributes.SetNamedItem(oAtt)
    Dim oAtt As Object = = xmldoc.CreateAttribute("DATATYPE")
    oAtt.Value = str(rs.Fields(x).Type.Name))
    oNode1.Attributes.SetNamedItem(oAtt)
    Dim oAtt As Object = = xmldoc.CreateAttribute("SIZE")
    oAtt.Value = str(rs.Fields(x).Value.)
    oNode1.Attributes.SetNamedItem(oAtt)
    Dim oAtt As Object = = xmldoc.CreateAttribute("Value")
    oAtt.Value = GetValue(prop, obj)
    oNode1.Attributes.SetNamedItem(oAtt)
    oNode.AppendChild(oNode1)
  Next
  oRoot.AppendChild(oNode)
Loop
xmldoc.AppendChild(oRoot)
Dim ws As Object =  CreateObject("WScript.Shell")
xmldoc.Save(ws.CurrentDirectory + "\\Products.xml")
```

ELEMENT XML USING A TEXT FILE

```
Dim ws As Object =  CreateObject("WScript.Shell")
Dim fso As Object =  CreateObject("Scripting.FileSystemObject")
Dim txtstream As Object =fso.OpenTextFile(ws.CurrentDirectory + "\Products.txt", 2, true, -2)
txtstream.WriteLine("<?xml version='1.0' encoding='iso-8859-1'?>")
txtstream.WriteLine("<data>")
rs.MoveFirst
Do While(rs.EOF = false)
  txtstream.WriteLine("<Products>")
  For x = 0 to rs.Fields.Count-1
    txtstream.WriteLine("<" + rs.Fields(x).Name + ">" + rs.Fields(x).Value + "</" + rs.Fields(x).Name + ">")
  Next
  txtstream.WriteLine("</Products>")
  rs.MoveNext()
Loop
txtstream.WriteLine("</data>")
txtstream.close()
```

ELEMENT XML USING THE DOM

```
Dim xmldoc as Object   = CreateObject("MSXML2.DOMDocument")
  Dim pi As Object = xmldoc.CreateProcessingInstruction("xml",
"version='1.0' encoding='ISO-8859-1'")

Dim oRoot As Object  = xmldoc.CreateElement("data")
xmldoc.AppendChild(pi)
Do While rs.EOF  = false
    Dim oNode As Object  = xmldoc.CreateNode(1, "Products", "")
  for x = 0 to rs.Fields.Count -1
       Dim oNode1 As Object = xmldoc.CreateNode(1, rs.Fields(x),Name, "")
       oNode1.Text = str(rs.Fields(x).Value)
       Call oNode.AppendChild(oNode1)
  Next
  Call oRoot.AppendChild(oNode)
  rs.MoveNext
Loop
```

```
Call xmldoc.AppendChild(oRoot)
Dim ws As Object =  CreateObject("WScript.Shell")
xmldoc.Save(ws.CurrentDirectory + "\\Products.xml")
```

ELEMENT XML FOR XSL USING A TEXT FILE

```
Dim ws As Object =  CreateObject("WScript.Shell")
Dim fso As Object =  CreateObject("Scripting.FileSystemObject")
Dim txtstream As Object =fso.OpenTextFile(ws.CurrentDirectory + "\Products.txt", 2, true, -2)
txtstream.WriteLine("<?xml version='1.0' encoding='iso-8859-1'?>")
txtstream.WriteLine("<?xml-stylesheet type='Text/xsl' href='" + ws.CurrentDirectory + "\Products.xsl"?>
txtstream.WriteLine("<?xml version='1.0' encoding='iso-8859-1'?>")
txtstream.WriteLine("<data>")
rs.MoveFirst
Do While(rs.EOF = false)
   txtstream.WriteLine("<Products>")
   For x = 0 to rs.Fields.Count-1
      txtstream.WriteLine("<" + rs.Fields(x).Name + ">" + rs.Fields(x).Value + "</" + rs.Fields(x).Name + ">")
   Next
   txtstream.WriteLine("</Products>")
   rs.MoveNext()
Loop
txtstream.WriteLine("</data>")
txtstream.close()
```

ELEMENT XML FOR XSL USING THE DOM

```
Dim xmldoc as Object   = CreateObject("MSXML2.DOMDocument")
  Dim pi As Object = xmldoc.CreateProcessingInstruction("xml", "version='1.0' encoding='ISO-8859-1'")
Dim pii As Object xmldoc.CreateProcessingInstruction("xml-stylesheet", "type='text/xsl' href='Process.xsl'")
Dim oRoot As Object  = xmldoc.CreateElement("data")
xmldoc.AppendChild(pi)
```

```
xmldoc.AppendChild(pii)
Do While rs.EOF  = false
     Dim oNode As Object  = xmldoc.CreateNode(1, "Products", "")
   for x = 0 to rs.Fields.Count -1
      Dim oNode1 As Object = xmldoc.CreateNode(1, rs.Fields(x),Name, "")
      oNode1.Text = str(rs.Fields(x).Value)
      Call oNode.AppendChild(oNode1)
   Next
   Call oRoot.AppendChild(oNode)
   rs.MoveNext
Loop
Call xmldoc.AppendChild(oRoot)
Dim ws As Object =  CreateObject("WScript.Shell")
xmldoc.Save(ws.CurrentDirectory + "\\Products.xml")
```

SCHEMA XML USING A TEXT FILE

```
   Dim ws As Object =  CreateObject("WScript.Shell")
   Dim fso As Object =  CreateObject("Scripting.FileSystemObject")
   Dim    txtstream    As    Object    =fso.OpenTextFile(ws.CurrentDirectory    +
"\Products.txt", 2, true, -2)
   txtstream.WriteLine("<?xml version='1.0' encoding='iso-8859-1'?>")
   txtstream.WriteLine("<data>")
   rs.MoveFirst
   Do While(rs.EOF = false)
      txtstream.WriteLine("<Products>")
      For x = 0 to rs.Fields.Count-1
         txtstream.WriteLine("<" + rs.Fields(x).Name + ">" + rs.Fields(x).Value +
"</" + rs.Fields(x).Name + ">")
      Next
      txtstream.WriteLine("</Products>")
      rs.MoveNext()
   Loop
   txtstream.WriteLine("</data>")
   txtstream.close()
   rs1 = CreateObject("ADODB.Recordset")
```

```
    rs1.ActiveConnection = "Provider=MSDAOSP; Data
Source=msxml2.DSOControl"
    rs1.Open(ws.CurrentDirectory + "\Products.xml")

    If (fso.FileExists(ws.CurrentDirectory + "\Products_Schema.xml") = true)
Then
      fso.DeleteFile(ws.CurrentDirectory + "\Products_Schema.xml")


    rs.Save(ws.CurrentDirectory + "\Products_Schema.xml", 1)
```

SCHEMA XML USING THE DOM

```
    Dim xmldoc as Object  = CreateObject("MSXML2.DOMDocument")
      Dim pi As Object = xmldoc.CreateProcessingInstruction("xml",
   "version='1.0' encoding='ISO-8859-1'")
    Dim oRoot As Object  = xmldoc.CreateElement("data")
    xmldoc.AppendChild(pi)
    Do While rs.EOF  = false
        Dim oNode As Object  = xmldoc.CreateNode(1, "Products", "")
      for x = 0 to rs.Fields.Count -1
          Dim oNode1 As Object = xmldoc.CreateNode(1, rs.Fields(x),Name, "")
          oNode1.Text = str(rs.Fields(x).Value)
          Call oNode.AppendChild(oNode1)
      Next
      Call oRoot.AppendChild(oNode)
      rs.MoveNext
    Loop
    Call xmldoc.AppendChild(oRoot)
    Dim ws As Object =  CreateObject("WScript.Shell")
    xmldoc.Save(ws.CurrentDirectory + "\\Products.xml")



    Dim rs1 As Object = CreateObject("ADODB.Recordset")
    rs1.ActiveConnection = "Provider=MSDAOSP; Data
Source=msxml2.DSOControl"
    rs1.Open(ws.CurrentDirectory + "\Products.xml")
```

```
    If (fso.FileExists(ws.CurrentDirectory + "\Products_Schema.xml") = true)
Then
      fso.DeleteFile(ws.CurrentDirectory + "\Products_Schema.xml")


    rs.Save(ws.CurrentDirectory + "\Products_Schema.xml", 1)
```

EXCEL CODING EXAMPLES

BELOW ARE SOME EXAMPLES OF ADO DRIVING EXCEL VISUAL RENDERINGS.

EXCEL CODE IN HORIZONTAL FORMAT USING A CSV FILE

```
Dim ws As Object = CreateObject("WScript.Shell")
Dim fso As Object = CreateObject("Scripting.FileSystemObject")
Dim txtstream As Object =fso.OpenTextFile(ws.CurrentDirectory + "\Products.csv", 2, true, -2)
tstr= ""


For x = 0 to rs.Fields.Count-1
   if tstr <> "" Then
      tstr = tstr + ","
   End If
   tstr = tstr + rs.Fields(x).Name
Next
txtstream.Writeline(tstr)
tstr = ""
```

```
rs.MoveFirst()
Do While(rs.EOF = false)
   For x = 0 to rs.Fields.Count-1
      if tstr <> "" Then
         tstr = tstr + ","
      End If
      tstr = tstr + chr(34) + rs.Fields(x).Value + chr(34)
   Next
   txtstream.Writeline(tstr)
   tstr = ""
   rs.MoveNext
Loop
```

EXCEL CODE IN VERTICAL FORMAT USING A CSV FILE

```
Dim ws As Object =  CreateObject("WScript.Shell")
Dim fso As Object =  CreateObject("Scripting.FileSystemObject")
Dim txtstream As Object =fso.OpenTextFile(ws.CurrentDirectory +
"\Products.csv", 2, true, -2)
tstr= ""
For x = 0 to rs.Fields.Count-1
   tstr = rs.Fields(x).Name
   rs.MoveFirst()
   Do While(rs.EOF = false)
      if tstr <> "" Then
         tstr = tstr + ","
      End If
      tstr = tstr + chr(34) + rs.Fields(x).Value + chr(34)
      rs.MoveNext
   Loop
   txtstream.Writeline(tstr)
   tstr = ""
Next
txtstream.Close

ws.Run(ws.CurrentDirectory + "\Products.csv")
```

EXCEL USING HORIZONTAL FORMAT AUTOMATION CODE

```
Dim oExcel As Object = CreateObject("Excel.Application")
oExcel.Visible = true
Dim wb As Object  As Object = oExcel.Workbooks.Add()
Dim ws As Object =  wb.WorkSheets(1)
ws.Name = "Products"
y=2
For x = 0 to rs.Fields.Count-1
   ws.Cells.Item(1, x+1) = rs.Fields(x).Name
Next
rs.MoveFirst()
Do While rs.EOF = False
   For x = 0 to rs.Fields.Count-1
      ws.Cells.Item(y, x +1) = rs.Fields(x).Value
   Next
   y=y+1
   rs.MoveNext
Loop

ws.Columns.HorizontalAlignment = -4131
iret = ws.Columns.AutoFit()
```

EXCEL USING VERTICAL FORMAT AUTOMATION CODE

```
oExcel = CreateObject("Excel.Application")
oExcel.Visible = true
wb = oExcel.Workbooks.Add()
Dim ws As Object =  wb.WorkSheets(1)
ws.Name = "Products"
y=2
For x = 0 to rs.Fields.Count-1
   ws.Cells.Item(x+1, 1) = rs.Fields(x).Name
Next
rs.MoveFirst()
Do While rs.EOF = False
   For x = 0 to rs.Fields.Count-1
      ws.Cells.Item(x +1, y) = rs.Fields(x).Value
```

```
    Next
    y=y+1
    rs.MoveNext
Loop

ws.Columns.HorizontalAlignment = -4131
iret = ws.Columns.AutoFit()
```

EXCEL SPREADSHEET EXAMPLE

```
Dim ws As Object = CreateObject("WScript.Shell")
Dim fso As Object = CreateObject("Scripting.FileSystemObject")
Dim txtstream As Object =fso.OpenTextFile(ws.CurrentDirectory + "\\ProcessExcel.xml", 2, true, -2)
txtstream.WriteLine("<?xml version='1.0'?>")
txtstream.WriteLine("<?mso-application progid='Excel.Sheet'?>")
txtstream.WriteLine("<Workbook xmlns='urn:schemas-microsoft-com:office:spreadsheet' xmlns:o='urn:schemas-microsoft-com:office:office' xmlns:x='urn:schemas-microsoft-com:office:excel' xmlns:ss='urn:schemas-microsoft-com:office:spreadsheet' xmlns:html='http://www.w3.org/TR/REC-html40'>")
txtstream.WriteLine(" <DocumentProperties xmlns='urn:schemas-microsoft-com:office:office'>")
txtstream.WriteLine("      <Author>Windows User</Author>")
txtstream.WriteLine("      <LastAuthor>Windows User</LastAuthor>")
txtstream.WriteLine("      <Created>2007-11-27T19:36:16Z</Created>")
txtstream.WriteLine("      <Version>12.00</Version>")
txtstream.WriteLine(" </DocumentProperties>")
txtstream.WriteLine(" <ExcelWorkbook xmlns='urn:schemas-microsoft-com:office:excel'>")
txtstream.WriteLine("      <WindowHeight>11835</WindowHeight>")
txtstream.WriteLine("      <WindowWidth>18960</WindowWidth>")
txtstream.WriteLine("      <WindowTopX>120</WindowTopX>")
txtstream.WriteLine("      <WindowTopY>135</WindowTopY>")
txtstream.WriteLine("      <ProtectStructure>False</ProtectStructure>")
txtstream.WriteLine("      <ProtectWindows>False</ProtectWindows>")
```

```
    txtstream.WriteLine("  </ExcelWorkbook>")
    txtstream.WriteLine("  <Styles>")
    txtstream.WriteLine("             <Style ss:ID='Default' ss:Name='Normal'>")
    txtstream.WriteLine("                          <Alignment ss:Vertical='Bottom'/>")
    txtstream.WriteLine("                          <Borders/>")
    txtstream.WriteLine("                          <Font              ss:FontName='Calibri'
x:Family='Swiss' ss:Size='11' ss:Color='#000000'/>")
    txtstream.WriteLine("                          <Interior/>")
    txtstream.WriteLine("                          <NumberFormat/>")
    txtstream.WriteLine("                          <Protection/>")
    txtstream.WriteLine("             </Style>")
    txtstream.WriteLine("             <Style ss:ID='s62'>")
    txtstream.WriteLine("                          <Borders/>")
    txtstream.WriteLine("                          <Font              ss:FontName='Calibri'
x:Family='Swiss' ss:Size='11' ss:Color='#000000' ss:Bold='1'/>")
    txtstream.WriteLine("             </Style>")
    txtstream.WriteLine("             <Style ss:ID='s63'>")
    txtstream.WriteLine("                          <Alignment          ss:Horizontal='Left'
ss:Vertical='Bottom' ss:Indent='2'/>")
    txtstream.WriteLine("                          <Font            ss:FontName='Verdana'
x:Family='Swiss' ss:Size='7.7' ss:Color='#000000'/>")
    txtstream.WriteLine("             </Style>")
    txtstream.WriteLine("   </Styles>")
    txtstream.WriteLine("<Worksheet ss:Name='Process'>")
    txtstream.WriteLine("              <Table     x:FullColumns='1'     x:FullRows='1'
ss:DefaultRowHeight='24.9375'>")
    txtstream.WriteLine("              <Column   ss:AutoFitWidth='1'   ss:Width='82.5'
ss:Span='5'/>")
    txtstream.WriteLine("      <Row ss:AutoFitHeight='0'>")
    For x = 0 To rs.Fields.Count-1
        txtstream.WriteLine("                           <Cell   ss:StyleID='s62'><Data
ss:Type='String'>" + rs.Fields(x).Name + "</Data></Cell>")
    Next
    txtstream.WriteLine("      </Row>")
    Do While rs.EOF = false
      txtstream.WriteLine("      <Row ss:AutoFitHeight='0' ss:Height='13.5'>")
      For x = 0 To rs.Fields.Count-1
        txtstream.WriteLine("            <Cell><Data ss:Type='String'><!(CDATA(" +
str(rs.Fields(x).Value)) + "))></Data></Cell>")
      Next
```

```
        txtstream.WriteLine("      </Row>")
        rs.MoveNext()
    Loop
    txtstream.WriteLine("  </Table>")
    txtstream.WriteLine(" <WorksheetOptions        xmlns='urn:schemas-microsoft-
com:office:excel'>")
    txtstream.WriteLine("            <PageSetup>")
    txtstream.WriteLine("                        <Header x:Margin='0.3'/>")
    txtstream.WriteLine("                        <Footer x:Margin='0.3'/>")
    txtstream.WriteLine("                        <PageMargins            x:Bottom='0.75'
x:Left='0.7' x:Right='0.7' x:Top='0.75'/>")
    txtstream.WriteLine("            </PageSetup>")
    txtstream.WriteLine("            <Unsynced/>")
    txtstream.WriteLine("            <Print>")
    txtstream.WriteLine("                        <FitHeight>0</FitHeight>")
    txtstream.WriteLine("                        <ValidPrinterInfo/>")
    txtstream.WriteLine("
          <HorizontalResolution>600</HorizontalResolution>")
    txtstream.WriteLine("
          <VerticalResolution>600</VerticalResolution>")
    txtstream.WriteLine("            </Print>")
    txtstream.WriteLine("            <Selected/>")
    txtstream.WriteLine("            <Panes>")
    txtstream.WriteLine("                        <Pane>")
    txtstream.WriteLine("                                    <Number>3</Number>")
    txtstream.WriteLine("                                    <ActiveRow>9</ActiveRow>")
    txtstream.WriteLine("                                    <ActiveCol>7</ActiveCol>")
    txtstream.WriteLine("                        </Pane>")
    txtstream.WriteLine("            </Panes>")
    txtstream.WriteLine("            <ProtectObjects>False</ProtectObjects>")
    txtstream.WriteLine("            <ProtectScenarios>False</ProtectScenarios>")
    txtstream.WriteLine(" </WorksheetOptions>")
    txtstream.WriteLine("</Worksheet>")
    txtstream.WriteLine("</Workbook>")
    txtstream.Close()
    ws.Run(ws.CurrentDirectory + "\\Products.xml")
```

CREATING XSL FILES

BELOW are examples of creating XSL files.

```
Dim ws As Object = CreateObject("WScript.Shell")
Dim fso As Object = CreateObject("Scripting.FileSystemObject")
Dim txtstream As Object =fso.OpenTextFile(ws.CurrentDirectory + "\Products.xsl", 2, true, -2)
txtstream.WriteLine("<?xml version='1.0' encoding='UTF-8'?>")
txtstream.WriteLine("<xsl:stylesheet version='1.0' xmlns:xsl='http://www.w3.org/1999/XSL/Transform'>")
txtstream.WriteLine("<xsl:template match=""/"">")
txtstream.WriteLine("<html>")
txtstream.WriteLine("<head>")
txtstream.WriteLine("<title>Products</title>")
txtstream.WriteLine("</head>")
#Add Stylesheet Here
txtstream.WriteLine("<body>")
rs.MoveFirst()
```

SINGLE LINE HORIZONTAL REPORTS

```
txtstream.WriteLine("<table border='0' Cellpadding='2' cellspacing='2>")
```

```
txtstream.WriteLine("<tr>")
for x = 0 to rs.Fields.count-1
   txtstream.WriteLine("<th align='left' nowrap='true'>" + rs.Fields(x).Name + "</th>")
Next
```

```
txtstream.WriteLine("</tr>")
txtstream.WriteLine("<tr>")
for x = 0 to rs.Fields.count-1
```

NONE

```
txtstream.WriteLine("<td><xsl:value-of select=""data/Products/" + rs.Fields(x).Name + """/></td>")
```

BUTTON

```
txtstream.WriteLine("<td align='left' nowrap='true'><button style='width:100%;'><xsl:value-of select=""data/Products/" + rs.Fields(x).Name + """/></button></td>")
```

COMBOBOX

```
txtstream.WriteLine("<td align='left' nowrap='true'><select><option><xsl:attribute name='value'><xsl:value-of select=""data/Products/" + rs.Fields(x).Name + """/></xsl:attribute><xsl:value-of select=""data/Products/" + rs.Fields(x).Name + """/></option></select></td>")
```

DIV

```
txtstream.WriteLine("<td align='left' nowrap='true'><div><xsl:value-of select=""data/Products/" + rs.Fields(x).Name + """/></div></td>")
```

LINK

```
txtstream.WriteLine("<td align='left' nowrap='true'><a href='" + rs.Fields(x).Value + "'><xsl:value-of select=""data/Products/" + rs.Fields(x).Name + """/></a></td>")
```

LISTBOX

```
txtstream.WriteLine("<td align='left' nowrap='true'><select multiple><option><xsl:attribute name='value'><xsl:value-of
```

```
select=""data/Products/" + rs.Fields(x).Name + """/></xsl:attribute><xsl:value-of select=""data/Products/" + rs.Fields(x).Name + """/></option></select></td>")
```

SPAN

```
txtstream.WriteLine("<td align='left' nowrap='true'><span><xsl:value-of select=""data/Products/" + rs.Fields(x).Name + """/></span></td>")
```

TEXTAREA

```
txtstream.WriteLine("<td align='left' nowrap='true'><textarea><xsl:value-of select=""data/Products/" + rs.Fields(x).Name + """/></textarea></td>")
```

TEXTBOX

```
txtstream.WriteLine("<td align='left' nowrap='true'><input type='text'><xsl:attribute name=""value""><xsl:value-of select=""data/Products/" + rs.Fields(x).Name + """/></xsl:attribute></input></td>")
    Next
    txtstream.WriteLine("</tr>")
    txtstream.WriteLine("</table>")
    txtstream.WriteLine("</body>")
    txtstream.WriteLine("</html>")
    txtstream.WriteLine("</xsl:template>")
    txtstream.WriteLine("</xsl:stylesheet>")
    txtstream.Close()
```

MULTI LINE HORIZONTAL REPORTS

```
txtstream.WriteLine("<table border='0' Cellpadding='2' cellspacing='2>")

    txtstream.WriteLine("<tr>")
    for x = 0 to rs.Fields.count-1
```

```
        txtstream.WriteLine("<th>" + rs.Fields(x).Name + "</th>")
    Next
    txtstream.WriteLine("</tr>")
    txtstream.WriteLine("<xsl:for-each select=""data/Products"">")
    txtstream.WriteLine("<tr>")
    for x = 0 to rs.Fields.count-1
        txtstream.WriteLine("<td><xsl:value-of select="" " + rs.Fields(x).Name + " ""/></td>")
```

NONE

```
        txtstream.WriteLine("<td><xsl:value-of select=""" + rs.Fields(x).Name + """/></td>")
```

BUTTON

```
        txtstream.WriteLine("<td align='left' nowrap='true'><button style='width:100%;'><xsl:value-of select=""" + rs.Fields(x).Name + """/></button></td>")
```

COMBOBOX

```
        txtstream.WriteLine("<td align='left' nowrap='true'><select><option><xsl:attribute name='value'><xsl:value-of select=""" + rs.Fields(x).Name + """/></xsl:attribute><xsl:value-of select=""data/Products/" + rs.Fields(x).Name + """/></option></select></td>")
```

DIV

```
        txtstream.WriteLine("<td align='left' nowrap='true'><div><xsl:value-of select=""data/Products/" + rs.Fields(x).Name + """/></div></td>")
```

LINK

```
        txtstream.WriteLine("<td align='left' nowrap='true'><a href='" + rs.Fields(x).Value + "'><xsl:value-of select=""data/Products/" + rs.Fields(x).Name + """/></a></td>")
```

LISTBOX

```
txtstream.WriteLine("<td align='left' nowrap='true'><select multiple><option><xsl:attribute name='value'><xsl:value-of select=""data/Products/" + rs.Fields(x).Name + """/></xsl:attribute><xsl:value-of select=""data/Products/" + rs.Fields(x).Name + """/></option></select></td>")
```

SPAN

```
txtstream.WriteLine("<td align='left' nowrap='true'><span><xsl:value-of select=""data/Products/" + rs.Fields(x).Name + """/></span></td>")
```

TEXTAREA

```
txtstream.WriteLine("<td align='left' nowrap='true'><textarea><xsl:value-of select=""data/Products/" + rs.Fields(x).Name + """/></textarea></td>")
```

TEXTBOX

```
txtstream.WriteLine("<td align='left' nowrap='true'><input type='text'><xsl:attribute name=""value""><xsl:value-of select=""data/Products/" + rs.Fields(x).Name + """/></xsl:attribute></input></td>")
    Next
    txtstream.WriteLine("</tr>")
    txtstream.WriteLine("</xsl:for-each>")
    txtstream.WriteLine("</table>")
    txtstream.WriteLine("</body>")
    txtstream.WriteLine("</html>")
    txtstream.WriteLine("</xsl:template>")
    txtstream.WriteLine("</xsl:stylesheet>")
    txtstream.Close()
```

SINGLE LINE VERTICAL REPORTS

```
for x = 0 to rs.Fields.count-1
   txtstream.WriteLine("<tr><th>" + rs.Fields(x).Name + "</th>")
```

NONE

```
txtstream.WriteLine("<td><xsl:value-of select=""data/Products/" + rs.Fields(x).Name + """/></td></tr>")
```

BUTTON

```
txtstream.WriteLine("<td align='left' nowrap='true'><button style='width:100%;'><xsl:value-of select=""data/Products/" + rs.Fields(x).Name + """/></button></td></tr>")
```

COMBOBOX

```
txtstream.WriteLine("<td align='left' nowrap='true'><select><option><xsl:attribute name='value'><xsl:value-of select=""data/Products/" + rs.Fields(x).Name + """/></xsl:attribute><xsl:value-of select=""data/Products/" + rs.Fields(x).Name + """/></option></select></td></tr>")
```

DIV

```
txtstream.WriteLine("<td align='left' nowrap='true'><div><xsl:value-of select=""data/Products/" + rs.Fields(x).Name + """/></div></td></tr>")
```

LINK

```
txtstream.WriteLine("<td align='left' nowrap='true'><a href='" + rs.Fields(x).Value + "'><xsl:value-of select=""data/Products/" + rs.Fields(x).Name + """/></a></td></tr>")
```

LISTBOX

```
txtstream.WriteLine("<td align='left' nowrap='true'><select multiple><option><xsl:attribute name='value'><xsl:value-of select=""data/Products/" + rs.Fields(x).Name + """/></xsl:attribute><xsl:value-of select=""data/Products/" + rs.Fields(x).Name + """/></option></select></td></tr>")
```

SPAN

```
txtstream.WriteLine("<td align='left' nowrap='true'><span><xsl:value-of select=""data/Products/" + rs.Fields(x).Name + """/></span></td></tr>")
```

TEXTAREA

```
txtstream.WriteLine("<td align='left' nowrap='true'><textarea><xsl:value-of select=""data/Products/" + rs.Fields(x).Name + """/></textarea></td></tr>")
```

TEXTBOX

```
txtstream.WriteLine("<td align='left' nowrap='true'><input type='text'><xsl:attribute name=""value""><xsl:value-of select=""data/Products/" + rs.Fields(x).Name + """/></xsl:attribute></input></td></tr>")

Next
txtstream.WriteLine("</table>")
txtstream.WriteLine("</body>")
txtstream.WriteLine("</html>")
txtstream.WriteLine("</xsl:template>")
txtstream.WriteLine("</xsl:stylesheet>")
txtstream.Close()
```

MULTI LINE VERTICAL REPORTS

```
txtstream.WriteLine("<table border='0' Cellpadding='2' cellspacing='2>")

for x = 0 to rs.Fields.count-1
    txtstream.WriteLine("<tr><th align='left' nowrap='true'>" + rs.Fields(x).Name + "</th>")
```

NONE

```
txtstream.WriteLine("<xsl:for-each select=""data/Products""><td align='left' nowrap='true'><xsl:value-of select=""" + rs.Fields(x).Name + """/></td></xsl:for-each></tr>")
```

BUTTON

```
txtstream.WriteLine("<xsl:for-each select=""data/Products""><td align='left' nowrap='true'><button style='width:100%;'><xsl:value-of select=""" + rs.Fields(x).Name + """/></button></td></xsl:for-each></tr>")
```

COMBOBOX

```
txtstream.WriteLine("<xsl:for-each select=""data/Products""><td align='left' nowrap='true'><select><option><xsl:attribute name='value'><xsl:value-of select=""" + rs.Fields(x).Name + """/></xsl:attribute><xsl:value-of select=""data/Products/" + rs.Fields(x).Name + """/></option></select></td></xsl:for-each></tr>")
```

DIV

```
txtstream.WriteLine("<xsl:for-each select=""data/Products""><td align='left' nowrap='true'><div><xsl:value-of select=""data/Products/" + rs.Fields(x).Name + """/></div></td></xsl:for-each></tr>")
```

LINK

```
txtstream.WriteLine("<xsl:for-each select=""data/Products""><td align='left' nowrap='true'><a href='" + rs.Fields(x).Value + "'><xsl:value-of select=""data/Products/" + rs.Fields(x).Name + """/></a></td></xsl:for-each></tr>")
```

LISTBOX

```
txtstream.WriteLine("<xsl:for-each select=""data/Products""><td align='left' nowrap='true'><select multiple><option><xsl:attribute name='value'><xsl:value-of select=""data/Products/" + rs.Fields(x).Name +
```

```
""""/></xsl:attribute><xsl:value-of select=""data/Products/" + rs.Fields(x).Name + """"/></option></select></td></xsl:for-each></tr>")
```

SPAN

```
txtstream.WriteLine("<xsl:for-each select=""data/Products""><td align='left' nowrap='true'><span><xsl:value-of select=""data/Products/" + rs.Fields(x).Name + """"/></span></td></xsl:for-each></tr>")
```

TEXTAREA

```
txtstream.WriteLine("<xsl:for-each select=""data/Products""><td align='left' nowrap='true'><textarea><xsl:value-of select=""data/Products/" + rs.Fields(x).Name + """"/></textarea></td></xsl:for-each></tr>")
```

TEXTBOX

```
txtstream.WriteLine("<xsl:for-each select=""data/Products""><td align='left' nowrap='true'><input type='text'><xsl:attribute name=""value""><xsl:value-of select=""data/Products/" + rs.Fields(x).Name + """"/></xsl:attribute></input></td></xsl:for-each></tr>")
```

```
Next
txtstream.WriteLine("</table>")
txtstream.WriteLine("</body>")
txtstream.WriteLine("</html>")
txtstream.WriteLine("</xsl:template>")
txtstream.WriteLine("</xsl:stylesheet>")
txtstream.Close()
```

SINGLE LINE HORIZONTAL TABLES

```
txtstream.WriteLine("<table style='border:Double;border-width:1px;border-color:navy;' rules=all frames=both cellpadding=2 cellspacing=2 Width=0>")

txtstream.WriteLine("<tr>")
```

```
for x = 0 to rs.Fields.count-1
    txtstream.WriteLine("<th align='left' nowrap='true'>" + rs.Fields(x).Name
+ "</th>")

txtstream.WriteLine("</tr>")
txtstream.WriteLine("<tr>")
for x = 0 to rs.Fields.count-1
```

NONE

```
    txtstream.WriteLine("<td><xsl:value-of select=""data/Products/" +
rs.Fields(x).Name + """/></td>")
```

BUTTON

```
        txtstream.WriteLine("<td align='left' nowrap='true'><button
style='width:100%;'><xsl:value-of select=""data/Products/" + rs.Fields(x).Name +
"""/></button></td>")
```

COMBOBOX

```
        txtstream.WriteLine("<td align='left'
nowrap='true'><select><option><xsl:attribute name='value'><xsl:value-of
select=""data/Products/" + rs.Fields(x).Name + """/></xsl:attribute><xsl:value-of
select=""data/Products/" + rs.Fields(x).Name + """/></option></select></td>")
```

DIV

```
        txtstream.WriteLine("<td align='left' nowrap='true'><div><xsl:value-of
select=""data/Products/" + rs.Fields(x).Name + """/></div></td>")
```

LINK

```
        txtstream.WriteLine("<td align='left' nowrap='true'><a href='" +
rs.Fields(x).Value + "'><xsl:value-of select=""data/Products/" + rs.Fields(x).Name
+ """/></a></td>")
```

LISTBOX

```
txtstream.WriteLine("<td align='left' nowrap='true'><select multiple><option><xsl:attribute name='value'><xsl:value-of select=""data/Products/" + rs.Fields(x).Name + """/></xsl:attribute><xsl:value-of select=""data/Products/" + rs.Fields(x).Name + """/></option></select></td>")
```

SPAN

```
txtstream.WriteLine("<td align='left' nowrap='true'><span><xsl:value-of select=""data/Products/" + rs.Fields(x).Name + """/></span></td>")
```

TEXTAREA

```
txtstream.WriteLine("<td align='left' nowrap='true'><textarea><xsl:value-of select=""data/Products/" + rs.Fields(x).Name + """/></textarea></td>")
```

TEXTBOX

```
txtstream.WriteLine("<td align='left' nowrap='true'><input type='text'><xsl:attribute name=""value""><xsl:value-of select=""data/Products/" + rs.Fields(x).Name + """/></xsl:attribute></input></td>")
```

```
Next
txtstream.WriteLine("</tr>")
txtstream.WriteLine("</table>")
txtstream.WriteLine("</body>")
txtstream.WriteLine("</html>")
txtstream.WriteLine("</xsl:template>")
txtstream.WriteLine("</xsl:stylesheet>")
txtstream.Close()
```

MULTI LINE HORIZONTAL TABLES

```
txtstream.WriteLine("<table style='border:Double;border-width:1px;border-color:navy;' rules=all frames=both cellpadding=2 cellspacing=2 Width=0>")
```

```
    txtstream.WriteLine("<tr>")
    for x = 0 to rs.Fields.count-1
      txtstream.WriteLine("<th>" + rs.Fields(x).Name + "</th>")
    Next
    txtstream.WriteLine("</tr>")
    txtstream.WriteLine("<xsl:for-each select=""data/Products"">")
    txtstream.WriteLine("<tr>")
    for x = 0 to rs.Fields.count-1
      txtstream.WriteLine("<td><xsl:value-of select="" " + rs.Fields(x).Name + "
""/></td>")
```

NONE

```
      txtstream.WriteLine("<td><xsl:value-of select=""" + rs.Fields(x).Name +
"""/></td>")
```

BUTTON

```
        txtstream.WriteLine("<td align='left' nowrap='true'><button
style='width:100%;'><xsl:value-of select=""" + rs.Fields(x).Name +
"""/></button></td>")
```

COMBOBOX

```
        txtstream.WriteLine("<td align='left'
nowrap='true'><select><option><xsl:attribute name='value'><xsl:value-of
select=""" + rs.Fields(x).Name + """/></xsl:attribute><xsl:value-of
select=""data/Products/" + rs.Fields(x).Name + """/></option></select></td>")
```

DIV

```
        txtstream.WriteLine("<td align='left' nowrap='true'><div><xsl:value-of
select=""data/Products/" + rs.Fields(x).Name + """/></div></td>")
```

LINK

```
txtstream.WriteLine("<td align='left' nowrap='true'><a href='" +
rs.Fields(x).Value + "'><xsl:value-of select=""data/Products/" + rs.Fields(x).Name
+ """/></a></td>")
```

LISTBOX

```
txtstream.WriteLine("<td align='left' nowrap='true'><select
multiple><option><xsl:attribute name='value'><xsl:value-of
select=""data/Products/" + rs.Fields(x).Name + """/></xsl:attribute><xsl:value-of
select=""data/Products/" + rs.Fields(x).Name + """/></option></select></td>")
```

SPAN

```
txtstream.WriteLine("<td align='left' nowrap='true'><span><xsl:value-
of select=""data/Products/" + rs.Fields(x).Name + """/></span></td>")
```

TEXTAREA

```
txtstream.WriteLine("<td align='left'
nowrap='true'><textarea><xsl:value-of select=""data/Products/" +
rs.Fields(x).Name + """/></textarea></td>")
```

TEXTBOX

```
txtstream.WriteLine("<td align='left' nowrap='true'><input
type='text'><xsl:attribute name=""value""><xsl:value-of select=""data/Products/"
+ rs.Fields(x).Name + """/></xsl:attribute></input></td>")
```

```
Next
txtstream.WriteLine("</tr>")
txtstream.WriteLine("</xsl:for-each>")
txtstream.WriteLine("</table>")
txtstream.WriteLine("</body>")
txtstream.WriteLine("</html>")
txtstream.WriteLine("</xsl:template>")
txtstream.WriteLine("</xsl:stylesheet>")
txtstream.Close()
```

```
for x = 0 to rs.Fields.count-1
    txtstream.WriteLine("<tr><th>" + rs.Fields(x).Name + "</th>")
```

NONE

```
txtstream.WriteLine("<td><xsl:value-of select=""data/Products/" + rs.Fields(x).Name + """/></td></tr>")
```

BUTTON

```
txtstream.WriteLine("<td align='left' nowrap='true'><button style='width:100%;'><xsl:value-of select=""data/Products/" + rs.Fields(x).Name + """/></button></td></tr>")
```

COMBOBOX

```
txtstream.WriteLine("<td align='left' nowrap='true'><select><option><xsl:attribute name='value'><xsl:value-of select=""data/Products/" + rs.Fields(x).Name + """/></xsl:attribute><xsl:value-of select=""data/Products/" + rs.Fields(x).Name + """/></option></select></td></tr>")
```

DIV

```
txtstream.WriteLine("<td align='left' nowrap='true'><div><xsl:value-of select=""data/Products/" + rs.Fields(x).Name + """/></div></td></tr>")
```

LINK

```
txtstream.WriteLine("<td align='left' nowrap='true'><a href='" + rs.Fields(x).Value + "'><xsl:value-of select=""data/Products/" + rs.Fields(x).Name + """/></a></td></tr>")
```

LISTBOX

```
txtstream.WriteLine("<td align='left' nowrap='true'><select multiple><option><xsl:attribute name='value'><xsl:value-of select=""data/Products/" + rs.Fields(x).Name + """/></xsl:attribute><xsl:value-of select=""data/Products/" + rs.Fields(x).Name + """/></option></select></td></tr>")
```

SPAN

```
txtstream.WriteLine("<td align='left' nowrap='true'><span><xsl:value-of select=""data/Products/" + rs.Fields(x).Name + """/></span></td></tr>")
```

TEXTAREA

```
txtstream.WriteLine("<td align='left' nowrap='true'><textarea><xsl:value-of select=""data/Products/" + rs.Fields(x).Name + """/></textarea></td></tr>")
```

TEXTBOX

```
txtstream.WriteLine("<td align='left' nowrap='true'><input type='text'><xsl:attribute name=""value""><xsl:value-of select=""data/Products/" + rs.Fields(x).Name + """/></xsl:attribute></input></td></tr>")
```

```
Next
txtstream.WriteLine("</table>")
txtstream.WriteLine("</body>")
txtstream.WriteLine("</html>")
txtstream.WriteLine("</xsl:template>")
txtstream.WriteLine("</xsl:stylesheet>")
txtstream.Close()
```

MULTI LINE VERTICAL TABLES

```
txtstream.WriteLine("<table style='border:Double;border-width:1px;border-color:navy;' rules=all frames=both cellpadding=2 cellspacing=2 Width=0>")
```

```
for x = 0 to rs.Fields.count-1
    txtstream.WriteLine("<tr><th align='left' nowrap='true'>" + rs.Fields(x).Name + "</th>")
```

NONE

```
    txtstream.WriteLine("<xsl:for-each select=""data/Products""><td align='left' nowrap='true'><xsl:value-of select=""" + rs.Fields(x).Name + """/></td></xsl:for-each></tr>")
```

BUTTON

```
    txtstream.WriteLine("<xsl:for-each select=""data/Products""><td align='left' nowrap='true'><button style='width:100%;'><xsl:value-of select=""" + rs.Fields(x).Name + """/></button></td></xsl:for-each></tr>")
```

COMBOBOX

```
    txtstream.WriteLine("<xsl:for-each select=""data/Products""><td align='left' nowrap='true'><select><option><xsl:attribute name='value'><xsl:value-of select=""" + rs.Fields(x).Name + """/></xsl:attribute><xsl:value-of select=""data/Products/" + rs.Fields(x).Name + """/></option></select></td></xsl:for-each></tr>")
```

DIV

```
    txtstream.WriteLine("<xsl:for-each select=""data/Products""><td align='left' nowrap='true'><div><xsl:value-of select=""data/Products/" + rs.Fields(x).Name + """/></div></td></xsl:for-each></tr>")
```

LINK

```
    txtstream.WriteLine("<xsl:for-each select=""data/Products""><td align='left' nowrap='true'><a href='" + rs.Fields(x).Value + "'><xsl:value-of
```

```
select=""data/Products/" + rs.Fields(x).Name + """/></a></td></xsl:for-each></tr>")
```

LISTBOX

```
txtstream.WriteLine("<xsl:for-each select=""data/Products""><td align='left' nowrap='true'><select multiple><option><xsl:attribute name='value'><xsl:value-of select=""data/Products/" + rs.Fields(x).Name + """/></xsl:attribute><xsl:value-of select=""data/Products/" + rs.Fields(x).Name + """/></option></select></td></xsl:for-each></tr>")
```

SPAN

```
txtstream.WriteLine("<xsl:for-each select=""data/Products""><td align='left' nowrap='true'><span><xsl:value-of select=""data/Products/" + rs.Fields(x).Name + """/></span></td></xsl:for-each></tr>")
```

TEXTAREA

```
txtstream.WriteLine("<xsl:for-each select=""data/Products""><td align='left' nowrap='true'><textarea><xsl:value-of select=""data/Products/" + rs.Fields(x).Name + """/></textarea></td></xsl:for-each></tr>")
```

TEXTBOX

```
txtstream.WriteLine("<xsl:for-each select=""data/Products""><td align='left' nowrap='true'><input type='text'><xsl:attribute name=""value""><xsl:value-of select=""data/Products/" + rs.Fields(x).Name + """/></xsl:attribute></input></td></xsl:for-each></tr>")
```

```
Next
txtstream.WriteLine("</table>")
txtstream.WriteLine("</body>")
txtstream.WriteLine("</html>")
txtstream.WriteLine("</xsl:template>")
txtstream.WriteLine("</xsl:stylesheet>")
txtstream.Close()
```

STYLESHEETS

Add some Pizzazz To your ASP, HTA, HTML and XSL pages

CSS turns okay into Amazing

BELOW is an assortment of stylesheets. There is nothing spectacular about them Just some ideas you can modify and put your own twist on them.

NONE

```
txtstream.WriteLine("<style type='text/css'>")
txtstream.WriteLine("th")
txtstream.WriteLine("{")
txtstream.WriteLine("    COLOR: Black;")
txtstream.WriteLine("}")
txtstream.WriteLine("td")
txtstream.WriteLine("{")
txtstream.WriteLine("    COLOR: Black;")
txtstream.WriteLine("}")
txtstream.WriteLine("</style>")
```

ITS A TABLE

```
txtstream.WriteLine("<style type='text/css'>")
txtstream.WriteLine("#itsthetable {")
txtstream.WriteLine("        font-family: Georgia, ""Times New Roman"",
Times, serif;")
txtstream.WriteLine("        color: #036;")
txtstream.WriteLine("}")
txtstream.WriteLine("caption {")
txtstream.WriteLine("        font-size: 48px;")
txtstream.WriteLine("        color: #036;")
txtstream.WriteLine("        font-weight: bolder;")
txtstream.WriteLine("        font-variant: small-caps;")
txtstream.WriteLine("}")
txtstream.WriteLine("th {")
txtstream.WriteLine("        font-size: 12px;")
txtstream.WriteLine("        color: #FFF;")
txtstream.WriteLine("        background-color: #06C;")
txtstream.WriteLine("        padding: 8px 4px;")
txtstream.WriteLine("        border-bottom: 1px solid #015ebc;")
txtstream.WriteLine("}")
txtstream.WriteLine("table {")
txtstream.WriteLine("        margin: 0;")
txtstream.WriteLine("        padding: 0;")
txtstream.WriteLine("        border-collapse: collapse;")
```

```
    txtstream.WriteLine("         border: 1px solid #06C;")
    txtstream.WriteLine("         width: 100%")
    txtstream.WriteLine("}")
    txtstream.WriteLine("#itsthetable th a:link, #itsthetable th a:visited {")
    txtstream.WriteLine("         color: #FFF;")
    txtstream.WriteLine("         text-decoration: none;")
    txtstream.WriteLine("         border-left: 5px solid #FFF;")
    txtstream.WriteLine("         padding-left: 3px;")
    txtstream.WriteLine("}")
    txtstream.WriteLine("th a:hover, #itsthetable th a:active {")
    txtstream.WriteLine("         color: #F90;")
    txtstream.WriteLine("         text-decoration: line-through;")
    txtstream.WriteLine("         border-left: 5px solid #F90;")
    txtstream.WriteLine("         padding-left: 3px;")
    txtstream.WriteLine("}")
    txtstream.WriteLine("tbody th:hover {")
    txtstream.WriteLine("         background-image:
url(imgs/tbody_hover.gif);")
    txtstream.WriteLine("         background-position: bottom;")
    txtstream.WriteLine("         background-repeat: repeat-x;")
    txtstream.WriteLine("}")
    txtstream.WriteLine("td {")
    txtstream.WriteLine("         background-color: #f2f2f2;")
    txtstream.WriteLine("         padding: 4px;")
    txtstream.WriteLine("         font-size: 12px;")
    txtstream.WriteLine("}")
    txtstream.WriteLine("#itsthetable td:hover {")
    txtstream.WriteLine("         background-color: #f8f8f8;")
    txtstream.WriteLine("}")
    txtstream.WriteLine("#itsthetable td a:link, #itsthetable td a:visited {")
    txtstream.WriteLine("         color: #039;")
    txtstream.WriteLine("         text-decoration: none;")
    txtstream.WriteLine("         border-left: 3px solid #039;")
    txtstream.WriteLine("         padding-left: 3px;")
    txtstream.WriteLine("}")
    txtstream.WriteLine("#itsthetable td a:hover, #itsthetable td a:active {")
    txtstream.WriteLine("         color: #06C;")
    txtstream.WriteLine("         text-decoration: line-through;")
    txtstream.WriteLine("         border-left: 3px solid #06C;")
    txtstream.WriteLine("         padding-left: 3px;")
```

```
txtstream.WriteLine("}")
txtstream.WriteLine("#itsthetable th {")
txtstream.WriteLine("        text-align: left;")
txtstream.WriteLine("        width: 150px;")
txtstream.WriteLine("}")
txtstream.WriteLine("#itsthetable tr {")
txtstream.WriteLine("        border-bottom: 1px solid #CCC;")
txtstream.WriteLine("}")
txtstream.WriteLine("#itsthetable thead th {")
txtstream.WriteLine("        background-image: url(imgs/thead_back.gif);")
txtstream.WriteLine("        background-repeat: repeat-x;")
txtstream.WriteLine("        background-color: #06C;")
txtstream.WriteLine("        height: 30px;")
txtstream.WriteLine("        font-size: 18px;")
txtstream.WriteLine("        text-align: center;")
txtstream.WriteLine("        text-shadow: #333 2px 2px;")
txtstream.WriteLine("        border: 2px;")
txtstream.WriteLine("}")
txtstream.WriteLine("#itsthetable tfoot th {")
txtstream.WriteLine("        background-image: url(imgs/tfoot_back.gif);")
txtstream.WriteLine("        background-repeat: repeat-x;")
txtstream.WriteLine("        background-color: #036;")
txtstream.WriteLine("        height: 30px;")
txtstream.WriteLine("        font-size: 28px;")
txtstream.WriteLine("        text-align: center;")
txtstream.WriteLine("        text-shadow: #333 2px 2px;")
txtstream.WriteLine("}")
txtstream.WriteLine("#itsthetable tfoot td {")
txtstream.WriteLine("        background-image: url(imgs/tfoot_back.gif);")
txtstream.WriteLine("        background-repeat: repeat-x;")
txtstream.WriteLine("        background-color: #036;")
txtstream.WriteLine("        color: FFF;")
txtstream.WriteLine("        height: 30px;")
txtstream.WriteLine("        font-size: 24px;")
txtstream.WriteLine("        text-align: left;")
txtstream.WriteLine("        text-shadow: #333 2px 2px;")
txtstream.WriteLine("}")
txtstream.WriteLine("tbody td a(href=""http://www.csslab.cl/"") {")
txtstream.WriteLine("        font-weight: bolder;")
txtstream.WriteLine("}")
```

```
txtstream.WriteLine("</style>")
```

BLACK AND WHITE TEXT

```
txtstream.WriteLine("<style type='text/css'>")
txtstream.WriteLine("th")
txtstream.WriteLine("{")
txtstream.WriteLine("   COLOR: white;")
txtstream.WriteLine("   BACKGROUND-COLOR: black;")
txtstream.WriteLine("   FONT-FAMILY: Cambria, serif;")
txtstream.WriteLine("   FONT-SIZE: 12px;")
txtstream.WriteLine("   text-align: left;")
txtstream.WriteLine("   white-Space: nowrap='nowrap';")
txtstream.WriteLine("}")
txtstream.WriteLine("td")
txtstream.WriteLine("{")
txtstream.WriteLine("   COLOR: white;")
txtstream.WriteLine("   BACKGROUND-COLOR: black;")
txtstream.WriteLine("   FONT-FAMILY: font-family: Cambria, serif;")
txtstream.WriteLine("   FONT-SIZE: 12px;")
txtstream.WriteLine("   text-align: left;")
txtstream.WriteLine("   white-Space: nowrap='nowrap';")
txtstream.WriteLine("}")
txtstream.WriteLine("div")
txtstream.WriteLine("{")
txtstream.WriteLine("   COLOR: white;")
txtstream.WriteLine("   BACKGROUND-COLOR: black;")
txtstream.WriteLine("   FONT-FAMILY: font-family: Cambria, serif;")
txtstream.WriteLine("   FONT-SIZE: 10px;")
txtstream.WriteLine("   text-align: left;")
txtstream.WriteLine("   white-Space: nowrap='nowrap';")
txtstream.WriteLine("}")
txtstream.WriteLine("span")
txtstream.WriteLine("{")
txtstream.WriteLine("   COLOR: white;")
txtstream.WriteLine("   BACKGROUND-COLOR: black;")
txtstream.WriteLine("   FONT-FAMILY: font-family: Cambria, serif;")
txtstream.WriteLine("   FONT-SIZE: 10px;")
```

```
txtstream.WriteLine("    text-align: left;")
txtstream.WriteLine("    white-Space: nowrap='nowrap';")
txtstream.WriteLine("    display:inline-block;")
txtstream.WriteLine("    width: 100%;")
txtstream.WriteLine("}")
txtstream.WriteLine("textarea")
txtstream.WriteLine("{")
txtstream.WriteLine("    COLOR: white;")
txtstream.WriteLine("    BACKGROUND-COLOR: black;")
txtstream.WriteLine("    FONT-FAMILY: font-family: Cambria, serif;")
txtstream.WriteLine("    FONT-SIZE: 10px;")
txtstream.WriteLine("    text-align: left;")
txtstream.WriteLine("    white-Space: nowrap='nowrap';")
txtstream.WriteLine("    width: 100%;")
txtstream.WriteLine("}")
txtstream.WriteLine("select")
txtstream.WriteLine("{")
txtstream.WriteLine("    COLOR: white;")
txtstream.WriteLine("    BACKGROUND-COLOR: black;")
txtstream.WriteLine("    FONT-FAMILY: font-family: Cambria, serif;")
txtstream.WriteLine("    FONT-SIZE: 10px;")
txtstream.WriteLine("    text-align: left;")
txtstream.WriteLine("    white-Space: nowrap='nowrap';")
txtstream.WriteLine("    width: 100%;")
txtstream.WriteLine("}")
txtstream.WriteLine("input")
txtstream.WriteLine("{")
txtstream.WriteLine("    COLOR: white;")
txtstream.WriteLine("    BACKGROUND-COLOR: black;")
txtstream.WriteLine("    FONT-FAMILY: font-family: Cambria, serif;")
txtstream.WriteLine("    FONT-SIZE: 12px;")
txtstream.WriteLine("    text-align: left;")
txtstream.WriteLine("    display:table-cell;")
txtstream.WriteLine("    white-Space: nowrap='nowrap';")
txtstream.WriteLine("}")
txtstream.WriteLine("h1 {")
txtstream.WriteLine("color: antiquewhite;")
txtstream.WriteLine("text-shadow: 1px 1px 1px black;")
txtstream.WriteLine("padding: 3px;")
txtstream.WriteLine("text-align: center;")
```

```
txtstream.WriteLine("box-shadow: in2px 2px 5px rgba(0,0,0,0.5), in-2px -2px 5px rgba(255,255,255,0.5);")
txtstream.WriteLine("}")
txtstream.WriteLine("</style>")
```

COLORED TEXT

```
txtstream.WriteLine("<style type='text/css'>")
txtstream.WriteLine("th")
txtstream.WriteLine("{")
txtstream.WriteLine("   COLOR: darkred;")
txtstream.WriteLine("   BACKGROUND-COLOR: #eeeeee;")
txtstream.WriteLine("   FONT-FAMILY: Cambria, serif;")
txtstream.WriteLine("   FONT-SIZE: 12px;")
txtstream.WriteLine("   text-align: left;")
txtstream.WriteLine("   white-Space: nowrap='nowrap';")
txtstream.WriteLine("}")
txtstream.WriteLine("td")
txtstream.WriteLine("{")
txtstream.WriteLine("   COLOR: navy;")
txtstream.WriteLine("   BACKGROUND-COLOR: #eeeeee;")
txtstream.WriteLine("   FONT-FAMILY: font-family: Cambria, serif;")
txtstream.WriteLine("   FONT-SIZE: 12px;")
txtstream.WriteLine("   text-align: left;")
txtstream.WriteLine("   white-Space: nowrap='nowrap';")
txtstream.WriteLine("}")
txtstream.WriteLine("div")
txtstream.WriteLine("{")
txtstream.WriteLine("   COLOR: white;")
txtstream.WriteLine("   BACKGROUND-COLOR: navy;")
txtstream.WriteLine("   FONT-FAMILY: font-family: Cambria, serif;")
txtstream.WriteLine("   FONT-SIZE: 10px;")
txtstream.WriteLine("   text-align: left;")
txtstream.WriteLine("   white-Space: nowrap='nowrap';")
txtstream.WriteLine("}")
txtstream.WriteLine("span")
txtstream.WriteLine("{")
txtstream.WriteLine("   COLOR: white;")
```

```
txtstream.WriteLine("    BACKGROUND-COLOR: navy;")
txtstream.WriteLine("    FONT-FAMILY: font-family: Cambria, serif;")
txtstream.WriteLine("    FONT-SIZE: 10px;")
txtstream.WriteLine("    text-align: left;")
txtstream.WriteLine("    white-Space: nowrap='nowrap';")
txtstream.WriteLine("    display:inline-block;")
txtstream.WriteLine("    width: 100%;")
txtstream.WriteLine("}")
txtstream.WriteLine("textarea")
txtstream.WriteLine("{")
txtstream.WriteLine("    COLOR: white;")
txtstream.WriteLine("    BACKGROUND-COLOR: navy;")
txtstream.WriteLine("    FONT-FAMILY: font-family: Cambria, serif;")
txtstream.WriteLine("    FONT-SIZE: 10px;")
txtstream.WriteLine("    text-align: left;")
txtstream.WriteLine("    white-Space: nowrap='nowrap';")
txtstream.WriteLine("    width: 100%;")
txtstream.WriteLine("}")
txtstream.WriteLine("select")
txtstream.WriteLine("{")
txtstream.WriteLine("    COLOR: white;")
txtstream.WriteLine("    BACKGROUND-COLOR: navy;")
txtstream.WriteLine("    FONT-FAMILY: font-family: Cambria, serif;")
txtstream.WriteLine("    FONT-SIZE: 10px;")
txtstream.WriteLine("    text-align: left;")
txtstream.WriteLine("    white-Space: nowrap='nowrap';")
txtstream.WriteLine("    width: 100%;")
txtstream.WriteLine("}")
txtstream.WriteLine("input")
txtstream.WriteLine("{")
txtstream.WriteLine("    COLOR: white;")
txtstream.WriteLine("    BACKGROUND-COLOR: navy;")
txtstream.WriteLine("    FONT-FAMILY: font-family: Cambria, serif;")
txtstream.WriteLine("    FONT-SIZE: 12px;")
txtstream.WriteLine("    text-align: left;")
txtstream.WriteLine("    display:table-cell;")
txtstream.WriteLine("    white-Space: nowrap='nowrap';")
txtstream.WriteLine("}")
txtstream.WriteLine("h1 {")
txtstream.WriteLine("color: antiquewhite;")
```

```
txtstream.WriteLine("text-shadow: 1px 1px 1px black;")
txtstream.WriteLine("padding: 3px;")
txtstream.WriteLine("text-align: center;")
txtstream.WriteLine("box-shadow: in2px 2px 5px rgba(0,0,0,0.5), in-2px -2px 5px rgba(255,255,255,0.5);")
txtstream.WriteLine("}")
txtstream.WriteLine("</style>")
```

OSCILLATING ROW COLORS

```
txtstream.WriteLine("<style type='text/css'>")
txtstream.WriteLine("th")
txtstream.WriteLine("{")
txtstream.WriteLine("    COLOR: white;")
txtstream.WriteLine("    BACKGROUND-COLOR: navy;")
txtstream.WriteLine("    FONT-FAMILY: Cambria, serif;")
txtstream.WriteLine("    FONT-SIZE: 12px;")
txtstream.WriteLine("    text-align: left;")
txtstream.WriteLine("    white-Space: nowrap='nowrap';")
txtstream.WriteLine("}")
txtstream.WriteLine("td")
txtstream.WriteLine("{")
txtstream.WriteLine("    COLOR: navy;")
txtstream.WriteLine("    FONT-FAMILY: font-family: Cambria, serif;")
txtstream.WriteLine("    FONT-SIZE: 12px;")
txtstream.WriteLine("    text-align: left;")
txtstream.WriteLine("    white-Space: nowrap='nowrap';")
txtstream.WriteLine("}")
txtstream.WriteLine("div")
txtstream.WriteLine("{")
txtstream.WriteLine("    COLOR: navy;")
txtstream.WriteLine("    FONT-FAMILY: font-family: Cambria, serif;")
txtstream.WriteLine("    FONT-SIZE: 12px;")
txtstream.WriteLine("    text-align: left;")
txtstream.WriteLine("    white-Space: nowrap='nowrap';")
txtstream.WriteLine("}")
txtstream.WriteLine("span")
txtstream.WriteLine("{")
```

```
txtstream.WriteLine("    COLOR: navy;")
txtstream.WriteLine("    FONT-FAMILY: font-family: Cambria, serif;")
txtstream.WriteLine("    FONT-SIZE: 12px;")
txtstream.WriteLine("    text-align: left;")
txtstream.WriteLine("    white-Space: nowrap='nowrap';")
txtstream.WriteLine("    width: 100%;")
txtstream.WriteLine("}")
txtstream.WriteLine("textarea")
txtstream.WriteLine("{")
txtstream.WriteLine("    COLOR: navy;")
txtstream.WriteLine("    FONT-FAMILY: font-family: Cambria, serif;")
txtstream.WriteLine("    FONT-SIZE: 12px;")
txtstream.WriteLine("    text-align: left;")
txtstream.WriteLine("    white-Space: nowrap='nowrap';")
txtstream.WriteLine("    display:inline-block;")
txtstream.WriteLine("    width: 100%;")
txtstream.WriteLine("}")
txtstream.WriteLine("select")
txtstream.WriteLine("{")
txtstream.WriteLine("    COLOR: navy;")
txtstream.WriteLine("    FONT-FAMILY: font-family: Cambria, serif;")
txtstream.WriteLine("    FONT-SIZE: 10px;")
txtstream.WriteLine("    text-align: left;")
txtstream.WriteLine("    white-Space: nowrap='nowrap';")
txtstream.WriteLine("    display:inline-block;")
txtstream.WriteLine("    width: 100%;")
txtstream.WriteLine("}")
txtstream.WriteLine("input")
txtstream.WriteLine("{")
txtstream.WriteLine("    COLOR: navy;")
txtstream.WriteLine("    FONT-FAMILY: font-family: Cambria, serif;")
txtstream.WriteLine("    FONT-SIZE: 12px;")
txtstream.WriteLine("    text-align: left;")
txtstream.WriteLine("    display:table-cell;")
txtstream.WriteLine("    white-Space: nowrap='nowrap';")
txtstream.WriteLine("}")
txtstream.WriteLine("h1 {")
txtstream.WriteLine("color: antiquewhite;")
txtstream.WriteLine("text-shadow: 1px 1px 1px black;")
txtstream.WriteLine("padding: 3px;")
```

```
txtstream.WriteLine("text-align: center;")
txtstream.WriteLine("box-shadow: in2px 2px 5px rgba(0,0,0,0.5), in-2px -
2px 5px rgba(255,255,255,0.5);")
txtstream.WriteLine("}")
txtstream.WriteLine("tr:nth-child(even){background-color:#f2f2f2;}")
txtstream.WriteLine("tr:nth-child(odd){background-color:#cccccc;
color:#f2f2f2;}")
txtstream.WriteLine("</style>")
```

GHOST DECORATED

```
txtstream.WriteLine("<style type='text/css'>")
txtstream.WriteLine("th")
txtstream.WriteLine("{")
txtstream.WriteLine("    COLOR: black;")
txtstream.WriteLine("    BACKGROUND-COLOR: white;")
txtstream.WriteLine("    FONT-FAMILY: Cambria, serif;")
txtstream.WriteLine("    FONT-SIZE: 12px;")
txtstream.WriteLine("    text-align: left;")
txtstream.WriteLine("    white-Space: nowrap='nowrap';")
txtstream.WriteLine("}")
txtstream.WriteLine("td")
txtstream.WriteLine("{")
txtstream.WriteLine("    COLOR: black;")
txtstream.WriteLine("    BACKGROUND-COLOR: white;")
txtstream.WriteLine("    FONT-FAMILY: font-family: Cambria, serif;")
txtstream.WriteLine("    FONT-SIZE: 12px;")
txtstream.WriteLine("    text-align: left;")
txtstream.WriteLine("    white-Space: nowrap='nowrap';")
txtstream.WriteLine("}")
txtstream.WriteLine("div")
txtstream.WriteLine("{")
txtstream.WriteLine("    COLOR: black;")
txtstream.WriteLine("    BACKGROUND-COLOR: white;")
txtstream.WriteLine("    FONT-FAMILY: font-family: Cambria, serif;")
txtstream.WriteLine("    FONT-SIZE: 10px;")
txtstream.WriteLine("    text-align: left;")
txtstream.WriteLine("    white-Space: nowrap='nowrap';")
```

```
txtstream.WriteLine("}")
txtstream.WriteLine("span")
txtstream.WriteLine("{")
txtstream.WriteLine("    COLOR: black;")
txtstream.WriteLine("    BACKGROUND-COLOR: white;")
txtstream.WriteLine("    FONT-FAMILY: font-family: Cambria, serif;")
txtstream.WriteLine("    FONT-SIZE: 10px;")
txtstream.WriteLine("    text-align: left;")
txtstream.WriteLine("    white-Space: nowrap='nowrap';")
txtstream.WriteLine("    display:inline-block;")
txtstream.WriteLine("    width: 100%;")
txtstream.WriteLine("}")
txtstream.WriteLine("textarea")
txtstream.WriteLine("{")
txtstream.WriteLine("    COLOR: black;")
txtstream.WriteLine("    BACKGROUND-COLOR: white;")
txtstream.WriteLine("    FONT-FAMILY: font-family: Cambria, serif;")
txtstream.WriteLine("    FONT-SIZE: 10px;")
txtstream.WriteLine("    text-align: left;")
txtstream.WriteLine("    white-Space: nowrap='nowrap';")
txtstream.WriteLine("    width: 100%;")
txtstream.WriteLine("}")
txtstream.WriteLine("select")
txtstream.WriteLine("{")
txtstream.WriteLine("    COLOR: black;")
txtstream.WriteLine("    BACKGROUND-COLOR: white;")
txtstream.WriteLine("    FONT-FAMILY: font-family: Cambria, serif;")
txtstream.WriteLine("    FONT-SIZE: 10px;")
txtstream.WriteLine("    text-align: left;")
txtstream.WriteLine("    white-Space: nowrap='nowrap';")
txtstream.WriteLine("    width: 100%;")
txtstream.WriteLine("}")
txtstream.WriteLine("input")
txtstream.WriteLine("{")
txtstream.WriteLine("    COLOR: black;")
txtstream.WriteLine("    BACKGROUND-COLOR: white;")
txtstream.WriteLine("    FONT-FAMILY: font-family: Cambria, serif;")
txtstream.WriteLine("    FONT-SIZE: 12px;")
txtstream.WriteLine("    text-align: left;")
txtstream.WriteLine("    display:table-cell;")
```

```
txtstream.WriteLine("    white-Space: nowrap='nowrap';")
txtstream.WriteLine("}")
txtstream.WriteLine("h1 {")
txtstream.WriteLine("color: antiquewhite;")
txtstream.WriteLine("text-shadow: 1px 1px 1px black;")
txtstream.WriteLine("padding: 3px;")
txtstream.WriteLine("text-align: center;")
txtstream.WriteLine("box-shadow: in2px 2px 5px rgba(0,0,0,0.5), in-2px -2px 5px rgba(255,255,255,0.5);")
txtstream.WriteLine("}")
txtstream.WriteLine("</style>")
```

3D

```
txtstream.WriteLine("<style type='text/css'>")
txtstream.WriteLine("body")
txtstream.WriteLine("{")
txtstream.WriteLine("    PADDING-RIGHT: 0px;")
txtstream.WriteLine("    PADDING-LEFT: 0px;")
txtstream.WriteLine("    PADDING-BOTTOM: 0px;")
txtstream.WriteLine("    MARGIN: 0px;")
txtstream.WriteLine("    COLOR: #333;")
txtstream.WriteLine("    PADDING-TOP: 0px;")
txtstream.WriteLine("    FONT-FAMILY: verdana, arial, helvetica, sans-serif;")
txtstream.WriteLine("}")
txtstream.WriteLine("table")
txtstream.WriteLine("{")
txtstream.WriteLine("    BORDER-RIGHT: #999999 3px solid;")
txtstream.WriteLine("    PADDING-RIGHT: 6px;")
txtstream.WriteLine("    PADDING-LEFT: 6px;")
txtstream.WriteLine("    FONT-WEIGHT: Bold;")
txtstream.WriteLine("    FONT-SIZE: 14px;")
txtstream.WriteLine("    PADDING-BOTTOM: 6px;")
txtstream.WriteLine("    COLOR: Peru;")
txtstream.WriteLine("    LINE-HEIGHT: 14px;")
txtstream.WriteLine("    PADDING-TOP: 6px;")
txtstream.WriteLine("    BORDER-BOTTOM: #999 1px solid;")
txtstream.WriteLine("    BACKGROUND-COLOR: #eeeeee;")
```

```
txtstream.WriteLine("    FONT-FAMILY: verdana, arial, helvetica, sans-serif;")
txtstream.WriteLine("    FONT-SIZE: 12px;")
txtstream.WriteLine("}")
txtstream.WriteLine("th")
txtstream.WriteLine("{")
txtstream.WriteLine("    BORDER-RIGHT: #999999 3px solid;")
txtstream.WriteLine("    PADDING-RIGHT: 6px;")
txtstream.WriteLine("    PADDING-LEFT: 6px;")
txtstream.WriteLine("    FONT-WEIGHT: Bold;")
txtstream.WriteLine("    FONT-SIZE: 14px;")
txtstream.WriteLine("    PADDING-BOTTOM: 6px;")
txtstream.WriteLine("    COLOR: darkred;")
txtstream.WriteLine("    LINE-HEIGHT: 14px;")
txtstream.WriteLine("    PADDING-TOP: 6px;")
txtstream.WriteLine("    BORDER-BOTTOM: #999 1px solid;")
txtstream.WriteLine("    BACKGROUND-COLOR: #eeeeee;")
txtstream.WriteLine("    FONT-FAMILY: Cambria, serif;")
txtstream.WriteLine("    FONT-SIZE: 12px;")
txtstream.WriteLine("    text-align: left;")
txtstream.WriteLine("    white-Space: nowrap='nowrap';")
txtstream.WriteLine("}")
txtstream.WriteLine(".th")
txtstream.WriteLine("{")
txtstream.WriteLine("    BORDER-RIGHT: #999999 2px solid;")
txtstream.WriteLine("    PADDING-RIGHT: 6px;")
txtstream.WriteLine("    PADDING-LEFT: 6px;")
txtstream.WriteLine("    FONT-WEIGHT: Bold;")
txtstream.WriteLine("    PADDING-BOTTOM: 6px;")
txtstream.WriteLine("    COLOR: black;")
txtstream.WriteLine("    PADDING-TOP: 6px;")
txtstream.WriteLine("    BORDER-BOTTOM: #999 2px solid;")
txtstream.WriteLine("    BACKGROUND-COLOR: #eeeeee;")
txtstream.WriteLine("    FONT-FAMILY: font-family: Cambria, serif;")
txtstream.WriteLine("    FONT-SIZE: 10px;")
txtstream.WriteLine("    text-align: right;")
txtstream.WriteLine("    white-Space: nowrap='nowrap';")
txtstream.WriteLine("}")
txtstream.WriteLine("td")
txtstream.WriteLine("{")
txtstream.WriteLine("    BORDER-RIGHT: #999999 3px solid;")
```

```
txtstream.WriteLine("   PADDING-RIGHT: 6px;")
txtstream.WriteLine("   PADDING-LEFT: 6px;")
txtstream.WriteLine("   FONT-WEIGHT: Normal;")
txtstream.WriteLine("   PADDING-BOTTOM: 6px;")
txtstream.WriteLine("   COLOR: navy;")
txtstream.WriteLine("   LINE-HEIGHT: 14px;")
txtstream.WriteLine("   PADDING-TOP: 6px;")
txtstream.WriteLine("   BORDER-BOTTOM: #999 1px solid;")
txtstream.WriteLine("   BACKGROUND-COLOR: #eeeeee;")
txtstream.WriteLine("   FONT-FAMILY: font-family: Cambria, serif;")
txtstream.WriteLine("   FONT-SIZE: 12px;")
txtstream.WriteLine("   text-align: left;")
txtstream.WriteLine("   white-Space: nowrap='nowrap';")
txtstream.WriteLine("}")
txtstream.WriteLine("div")
txtstream.WriteLine("{")
txtstream.WriteLine("   BORDER-RIGHT: #999999 3px solid;")
txtstream.WriteLine("   PADDING-RIGHT: 6px;")
txtstream.WriteLine("   PADDING-LEFT: 6px;")
txtstream.WriteLine("   FONT-WEIGHT: Normal;")
txtstream.WriteLine("   PADDING-BOTTOM: 6px;")
txtstream.WriteLine("   COLOR: white;")
txtstream.WriteLine("   PADDING-TOP: 6px;")
txtstream.WriteLine("   BORDER-BOTTOM: #999 1px solid;")
txtstream.WriteLine("   BACKGROUND-COLOR: navy;")
txtstream.WriteLine("   FONT-FAMILY: font-family: Cambria, serif;")
txtstream.WriteLine("   FONT-SIZE: 10px;")
txtstream.WriteLine("   text-align: left;")
txtstream.WriteLine("   white-Space: nowrap='nowrap';")
txtstream.WriteLine("}")
txtstream.WriteLine("span")
txtstream.WriteLine("{")
txtstream.WriteLine("   BORDER-RIGHT: #999999 3px solid;")
txtstream.WriteLine("   PADDING-RIGHT: 3px;")
txtstream.WriteLine("   PADDING-LEFT: 3px;")
txtstream.WriteLine("   FONT-WEIGHT: Normal;")
txtstream.WriteLine("   PADDING-BOTTOM: 3px;")
txtstream.WriteLine("   COLOR: white;")
txtstream.WriteLine("   PADDING-TOP: 3px;")
txtstream.WriteLine("   BORDER-BOTTOM: #999 1px solid;")
```

```
txtstream.WriteLine("    BACKGROUND-COLOR: navy;")
txtstream.WriteLine("    FONT-FAMILY: font-family: Cambria, serif;")
txtstream.WriteLine("    FONT-SIZE: 10px;")
txtstream.WriteLine("    text-align: left;")
txtstream.WriteLine("    white-Space: nowrap='nowrap';")
txtstream.WriteLine("    display:inline-block;")
txtstream.WriteLine("    width: 100%;")
txtstream.WriteLine("}")
txtstream.WriteLine("textarea")
txtstream.WriteLine("{")
txtstream.WriteLine("    BORDER-RIGHT: #999999 3px solid;")
txtstream.WriteLine("    PADDING-RIGHT: 3px;")
txtstream.WriteLine("    PADDING-LEFT: 3px;")
txtstream.WriteLine("    FONT-WEIGHT: Normal;")
txtstream.WriteLine("    PADDING-BOTTOM: 3px;")
txtstream.WriteLine("    COLOR: white;")
txtstream.WriteLine("    PADDING-TOP: 3px;")
txtstream.WriteLine("    BORDER-BOTTOM: #999 1px solid;")
txtstream.WriteLine("    BACKGROUND-COLOR: navy;")
txtstream.WriteLine("    FONT-FAMILY: font-family: Cambria, serif;")
txtstream.WriteLine("    FONT-SIZE: 10px;")
txtstream.WriteLine("    text-align: left;")
txtstream.WriteLine("    white-Space: nowrap='nowrap';")
txtstream.WriteLine("    width: 100%;")
txtstream.WriteLine("}")
txtstream.WriteLine("select")
txtstream.WriteLine("{")
txtstream.WriteLine("    BORDER-RIGHT: #999999 3px solid;")
txtstream.WriteLine("    PADDING-RIGHT: 6px;")
txtstream.WriteLine("    PADDING-LEFT: 6px;")
txtstream.WriteLine("    FONT-WEIGHT: Normal;")
txtstream.WriteLine("    PADDING-BOTTOM: 6px;")
txtstream.WriteLine("    COLOR: white;")
txtstream.WriteLine("    PADDING-TOP: 6px;")
txtstream.WriteLine("    BORDER-BOTTOM: #999 1px solid;")
txtstream.WriteLine("    BACKGROUND-COLOR: navy;")
txtstream.WriteLine("    FONT-FAMILY: font-family: Cambria, serif;")
txtstream.WriteLine("    FONT-SIZE: 10px;")
txtstream.WriteLine("    text-align: left;")
txtstream.WriteLine("    white-Space: nowrap='nowrap';")
```

```
txtstream.WriteLine("    width: 100%;")
txtstream.WriteLine("}")
txtstream.WriteLine("input")
txtstream.WriteLine("{")
txtstream.WriteLine("    BORDER-RIGHT: #999999 3px solid;")
txtstream.WriteLine("    PADDING-RIGHT: 3px;")
txtstream.WriteLine("    PADDING-LEFT: 3px;")
txtstream.WriteLine("    FONT-WEIGHT: Bold;")
txtstream.WriteLine("    PADDING-BOTTOM: 3px;")
txtstream.WriteLine("    COLOR: white;")
txtstream.WriteLine("    PADDING-TOP: 3px;")
txtstream.WriteLine("    BORDER-BOTTOM: #999 1px solid;")
txtstream.WriteLine("    BACKGROUND-COLOR: navy;")
txtstream.WriteLine("    FONT-FAMILY: font-family: Cambria, serif;")
txtstream.WriteLine("    FONT-SIZE: 12px;")
txtstream.WriteLine("    text-align: left;")
txtstream.WriteLine("    display:table-cell;")
txtstream.WriteLine("    white-Space: nowrap='nowrap';")
txtstream.WriteLine("    width: 100%;")
txtstream.WriteLine("}")
txtstream.WriteLine("h1 {")
txtstream.WriteLine("color: antiquewhite;")
txtstream.WriteLine("text-shadow: 1px 1px 1px black;")
txtstream.WriteLine("padding: 3px;")
txtstream.WriteLine("text-align: center;")
txtstream.WriteLine("box-shadow: in2px 2px 5px rgba(0,0,0,0.5), in-2px -2px 5px rgba(255,255,255,0.5);")
txtstream.WriteLine("}")
txtstream.WriteLine("</style>")
```

SHADOW BOX

```
txtstream.WriteLine("<style type='text/css'>")
txtstream.WriteLine("body")
txtstream.WriteLine("{")
txtstream.WriteLine("    PADDING-RIGHT: 0px;")
txtstream.WriteLine("    PADDING-LEFT: 0px;")
txtstream.WriteLine("    PADDING-BOTTOM: 0px;")
```

```
txtstream.WriteLine("    MARGIN: 0px;")
txtstream.WriteLine("    COLOR: #333;")
txtstream.WriteLine("    PADDING-TOP: 0px;")
txtstream.WriteLine("    FONT-FAMILY: verdana, arial, helvetica, sans-serif;")
txtstream.WriteLine("}")
txtstream.WriteLine("table")
txtstream.WriteLine("{")
txtstream.WriteLine("    BORDER-RIGHT: #999999 1px solid;")
txtstream.WriteLine("    PADDING-RIGHT: 1px;")
txtstream.WriteLine("    PADDING-LEFT: 1px;")
txtstream.WriteLine("    PADDING-BOTTOM: 1px;")
txtstream.WriteLine("    LINE-HEIGHT: 8px;")
txtstream.WriteLine("    PADDING-TOP: 1px;")
txtstream.WriteLine("    BORDER-BOTTOM: #999 1px solid;")
txtstream.WriteLine("    BACKGROUND-COLOR: #eeeeee;")
txtstream.WriteLine("
filter:progid:DXImageTransform.Microsoft.Shadow(color='silver', Direction=135,
Strength=16)")
txtstream.WriteLine("}")
txtstream.WriteLine("th")
txtstream.WriteLine("{")
txtstream.WriteLine("    BORDER-RIGHT: #999999 3px solid;")
txtstream.WriteLine("    PADDING-RIGHT: 6px;")
txtstream.WriteLine("    PADDING-LEFT: 6px;")
txtstream.WriteLine("    FONT-WEIGHT: Bold;")
txtstream.WriteLine("    FONT-SIZE: 14px;")
txtstream.WriteLine("    PADDING-BOTTOM: 6px;")
txtstream.WriteLine("    COLOR: darkred;")
txtstream.WriteLine("    LINE-HEIGHT: 14px;")
txtstream.WriteLine("    PADDING-TOP: 6px;")
txtstream.WriteLine("    BORDER-BOTTOM: #999 1px solid;")
txtstream.WriteLine("    BACKGROUND-COLOR: #eeeeee;")
txtstream.WriteLine("    FONT-FAMILY: font-family: Cambria, serif;")
txtstream.WriteLine("    FONT-SIZE: 12px;")
txtstream.WriteLine("    text-align: left;")
txtstream.WriteLine("    white-Space: nowrap='nowrap';")
txtstream.WriteLine("}")
txtstream.WriteLine(".th")
txtstream.WriteLine("{")
txtstream.WriteLine("    BORDER-RIGHT: #999999 2px solid;")
```

```
txtstream.WriteLine("    PADDING-RIGHT: 6px;")
txtstream.WriteLine("    PADDING-LEFT: 6px;")
txtstream.WriteLine("    FONT-WEIGHT: Bold;")
txtstream.WriteLine("    PADDING-BOTTOM: 6px;")
txtstream.WriteLine("    COLOR: black;")
txtstream.WriteLine("    PADDING-TOP: 6px;")
txtstream.WriteLine("    BORDER-BOTTOM: #999 2px solid;")
txtstream.WriteLine("    BACKGROUND-COLOR: #eeeeee;")
txtstream.WriteLine("    FONT-FAMILY: font-family: Cambria, serif;")
txtstream.WriteLine("    FONT-SIZE: 10px;")
txtstream.WriteLine("    text-align: right;")
txtstream.WriteLine("    white-Space: nowrap='nowrap';")
txtstream.WriteLine("}")
txtstream.WriteLine("td")
txtstream.WriteLine("{")
txtstream.WriteLine("    BORDER-RIGHT: #999999 3px solid;")
txtstream.WriteLine("    PADDING-RIGHT: 6px;")
txtstream.WriteLine("    PADDING-LEFT: 6px;")
txtstream.WriteLine("    FONT-WEIGHT: Normal;")
txtstream.WriteLine("    PADDING-BOTTOM: 6px;")
txtstream.WriteLine("    COLOR: navy;")
txtstream.WriteLine("    LINE-HEIGHT: 14px;")
txtstream.WriteLine("    PADDING-TOP: 6px;")
txtstream.WriteLine("    BORDER-BOTTOM: #999 1px solid;")
txtstream.WriteLine("    BACKGROUND-COLOR: #eeeeee;")
txtstream.WriteLine("    FONT-FAMILY: font-family: Cambria, serif;")
txtstream.WriteLine("    FONT-SIZE: 12px;")
txtstream.WriteLine("    text-align: left;")
txtstream.WriteLine("    white-Space: nowrap='nowrap';")
txtstream.WriteLine("}")
txtstream.WriteLine("div")
txtstream.WriteLine("{")
txtstream.WriteLine("    BORDER-RIGHT: #999999 3px solid;")
txtstream.WriteLine("    PADDING-RIGHT: 6px;")
txtstream.WriteLine("    PADDING-LEFT: 6px;")
txtstream.WriteLine("    FONT-WEIGHT: Normal;")
txtstream.WriteLine("    PADDING-BOTTOM: 6px;")
txtstream.WriteLine("    COLOR: white;")
txtstream.WriteLine("    PADDING-TOP: 6px;")
txtstream.WriteLine("    BORDER-BOTTOM: #999 1px solid;")
```

```
txtstream.WriteLine("    BACKGROUND-COLOR: navy;")
txtstream.WriteLine("    FONT-FAMILY: font-family: Cambria, serif;")
txtstream.WriteLine("    FONT-SIZE: 10px;")
txtstream.WriteLine("    text-align: left;")
txtstream.WriteLine("    white-Space: nowrap='nowrap';")
txtstream.WriteLine("}")
txtstream.WriteLine("span")
txtstream.WriteLine("{")
txtstream.WriteLine("    BORDER-RIGHT: #999999 3px solid;")
txtstream.WriteLine("    PADDING-RIGHT: 3px;")
txtstream.WriteLine("    PADDING-LEFT: 3px;")
txtstream.WriteLine("    FONT-WEIGHT: Normal;")
txtstream.WriteLine("    PADDING-BOTTOM: 3px;")
txtstream.WriteLine("    COLOR: white;")
txtstream.WriteLine("    PADDING-TOP: 3px;")
txtstream.WriteLine("    BORDER-BOTTOM: #999 1px solid;")
txtstream.WriteLine("    BACKGROUND-COLOR: navy;")
txtstream.WriteLine("    FONT-FAMILY: font-family: Cambria, serif;")
txtstream.WriteLine("    FONT-SIZE: 10px;")
txtstream.WriteLine("    text-align: left;")
txtstream.WriteLine("    white-Space: nowrap='nowrap';")
txtstream.WriteLine("    display: inline-block;")
txtstream.WriteLine("    width: 100%;")
txtstream.WriteLine("}")
txtstream.WriteLine("textarea")
txtstream.WriteLine("{")
txtstream.WriteLine("    BORDER-RIGHT: #999999 3px solid;")
txtstream.WriteLine("    PADDING-RIGHT: 3px;")
txtstream.WriteLine("    PADDING-LEFT: 3px;")
txtstream.WriteLine("    FONT-WEIGHT: Normal;")
txtstream.WriteLine("    PADDING-BOTTOM: 3px;")
txtstream.WriteLine("    COLOR: white;")
txtstream.WriteLine("    PADDING-TOP: 3px;")
txtstream.WriteLine("    BORDER-BOTTOM: #999 1px solid;")
txtstream.WriteLine("    BACKGROUND-COLOR: navy;")
txtstream.WriteLine("    FONT-FAMILY: font-family: Cambria, serif;")
txtstream.WriteLine("    FONT-SIZE: 10px;")
txtstream.WriteLine("    text-align: left;")
txtstream.WriteLine("    white-Space: nowrap='nowrap';")
txtstream.WriteLine("    width: 100%;")
```

```
txtstream.WriteLine("}")
txtstream.WriteLine("select")
txtstream.WriteLine("{")
txtstream.WriteLine("    BORDER-RIGHT: #999999 3px solid;")
txtstream.WriteLine("    PADDING-RIGHT: 6px;")
txtstream.WriteLine("    PADDING-LEFT: 6px;")
txtstream.WriteLine("    FONT-WEIGHT: Normal;")
txtstream.WriteLine("    PADDING-BOTTOM: 6px;")
txtstream.WriteLine("    COLOR: white;")
txtstream.WriteLine("    PADDING-TOP: 6px;")
txtstream.WriteLine("    BORDER-BOTTOM: #999 1px solid;")
txtstream.WriteLine("    BACKGROUND-COLOR: navy;")
txtstream.WriteLine("    FONT-FAMILY: font-family: Cambria, serif;")
txtstream.WriteLine("    FONT-SIZE: 10px;")
txtstream.WriteLine("    text-align: left;")
txtstream.WriteLine("    white-Space: nowrap='nowrap';")
txtstream.WriteLine("    width: 100%;")
txtstream.WriteLine("}")
txtstream.WriteLine("input")
txtstream.WriteLine("{")
txtstream.WriteLine("    BORDER-RIGHT: #999999 3px solid;")
txtstream.WriteLine("    PADDING-RIGHT: 3px;")
txtstream.WriteLine("    PADDING-LEFT: 3px;")
txtstream.WriteLine("    FONT-WEIGHT: Bold;")
txtstream.WriteLine("    PADDING-BOTTOM: 3px;")
txtstream.WriteLine("    COLOR: white;")
txtstream.WriteLine("    PADDING-TOP: 3px;")
txtstream.WriteLine("    BORDER-BOTTOM: #999 1px solid;")
txtstream.WriteLine("    BACKGROUND-COLOR: navy;")
txtstream.WriteLine("    FONT-FAMILY: font-family: Cambria, serif;")
txtstream.WriteLine("    FONT-SIZE: 12px;")
txtstream.WriteLine("    text-align: left;")
txtstream.WriteLine("    display: table-cell;")
txtstream.WriteLine("    white-Space: nowrap='nowrap';")
txtstream.WriteLine("    width: 100%;")
txtstream.WriteLine("}")
txtstream.WriteLine("h1 {")
txtstream.WriteLine("color: antiquewhite;")
txtstream.WriteLine("text-shadow: 1px 1px 1px black;")
txtstream.WriteLine("padding: 3px;")
```

```
txtstream.WriteLine("text-align: center;")
txtstream.WriteLine("box-shadow: in2px 2px 5px rgba(0,0,0,0.5), in-2px -2px 5px rgba(255,255,255,0.5);")
txtstream.WriteLine("}")
txtstream.WriteLine("</style>")
```

www.ingramcontent.com/pod-product-compliance
Lightning Source LLC
Chambersburg PA
CBHW070843070326
40690CB00009B/1669
9781720524885